Notes from the 48th North

Spotlight on a Stream of Consciousness

Isolde Martin

First published by Busybird Publishing 2016
Copyright © 2016 Isolde Martin

ISBN
978-0-9945322-4-4 (Print)
978-0-9945322-5-1 (Ebook)

Isolde Martin has asserted her right under the Copyright, Designs and Patents Act 1988 to be identified as the author of this work. The information in this book is based on the author's experiences and opinions. The publisher specifically disclaims responsibility for any adverse consequences, which may result from use of the information contained herein. Permission to use information has been sought by the author. Any breaches will be rectified in further editions of the book.

All rights reserved. No part of this publication may be reproduced, stored in or introduced into a retrieval system, or transmitted in any form, or by any means (electronic, mechanical, photocopying, recording or otherwise) without the prior written permission of the author. Any person who does any unauthorised act in relation to this publication may be liable to criminal prosecution and civil claims for damages. Inquiries should be made through the publisher.

Cover image: Luke Harris, Chameleon Design
Cover design: Busybird Publishing
Layout and typesetting: Busybird Publishing

Busybird Publishing
PO Box 855
Eltham Victoria
Australia 3095
www.busybird.com.au

Thank you note:
Dedicated to Les Zigomanis.
Without him this book would not exist.

Notes from the 48th North

Sent: Monday, 27 April 2009 ~ 10.13am

The morning sky is undecided. It is very dark in the West, gently leading over into gray and white clouds. The sun sends bright warm rays from the East. What, pray tell me, is the right thing to wear? Well, take an inner layer of "cool", a middle layer of "cool spring", an outer layer of "could be very cool and windy" and take an umbrella. Off we go downtown. As I come out of the forest I let the car go pretty slow so that I can watch the scenery. It is green, so mighty green, my mind rebels and thinks back to the brown-yellowish desert sand. But then there are the spring flowers in the meadows, yellow, white and blue. I am up high. The road runs along the rim of the hills. The alpine panorama on the southern horizon is beautiful, letting me see all the way into the Austrian Alps, and low and behold, there is still snow on the peaks! Suddenly I remember that I am driving a car. Pay attention, Isolde! Then the sky catches my eye. It is clearly blue now. I see three white stripes from three airplanes. And they are clearly going towards each other! Are they going to meet in the middle? I keep on glancing up into the air watching the path of the planes. Okay, they have passed over and under each other. Phew! Do not know how I made it into the city without driving off into a field!

Notes from the Pacific Rim

Sent: Tuesday, 12 May 2009 ~ 9.59am

Refreshing was Boulder, wonderful our son and delightful his friend. But tomorrow is time to go back to San Francisco to catch our flight to Munich. Why do we not fly from Denver, they ask, it is shorter. Yes, but it is cheaper to leave from the port you arrived, we explain. Frontier Airline will take us to SF. What a fitting name! But, the lady says, your flight to SF is at 9.00pm not am! What?! But then our flight to Munich will leave before we arrive?! Well, then we need to re-book. Here is one at 12.00 noon and with the time difference you can easily spend some time in that wonderful ocean pearl of a city still.

Yes, Steven says, this is great, for I need some San Francisco sourdough bread and I need to see whether the seals are still there. Take the cable car, and go to Fisherman's Wharf. I feel I am back home in the city that is part of my husband's identity, the city he loves, the bay area that he loves, the Pacific that is his ocean and the seals that indicate the health of that place. The seals have prevailed, defying in and outgoing vessels. The people of San Francisco have built platforms for them, so that they can take their place in the California sun in the middle of the harbor. Yes, there they are, as fat, healthy and beautiful as ever before. The world is still okay then. Now we can leave in peace for other destinations on the globe. It was worth it to go back to San Francisco, wasn't it?

Notes from the 48th North

Sent: Saturday, 25 July 2009 ~ 9.59am

It has rained and rained and has been cold. Now it has rained but is warm and damp. For our patience and endurance we even got rewarded with sunshine between two clouds. That is the right kind of weather to wear my tunica-style clothes. I have been waiting for that – with less patience. I had to go downtown that day, when the summer reminded us that it is waiting behind the clouds to come out. I wore my tight tights and my long sleeve, colorfully patterned, below hip-long top. Waiting for my husband to come out of his hairdresser's shop, I stumbled into one of my favourite shops for lingerie, bathing suits, pants, suits, etc. In short they have a small boutique, but the best. And their personnel also have the eyes of a profi. Where did you get that tunica-style top? So she asked pointedly. We have just ordered those and tight pants for next season. It is going to be theeeeee fashion next year. Oh is it then? I asked. Well I did not know, I am wearing it because I like it, fashion or not. Sensing that some other store was ahead of hers she inquired again: I have been looking at it when you came in. Who is carrying this already? With great pleasure, pride and glee I told her: I have it from my own Pakistani designer in Dubai! She was silent for a second or two and then answered: Oh! Soothingly I remarked that I pick up my pants next week then. Have a good day. *Auf Wiedersehen*!

I am afraid I am a bit on the snobbish side these days. Perhaps it compensates for going through enormous change.

Notes from the 48th North

Sent: Monday, 17 August 2009 ~ 11.25am

This is a beautiful morning all around – azure blue sky, warm, clear air, slight breeze. I call Uschi who sometimes is my walking partner. But she has already gone somewhere, her daughter says. Pity, I do not like to walk cross country between fields of corn which is higher than me. Things have happened to women that way. But I decide to brave it and go. I take my hat, my fending-off FIFO device, and my mobile. I pass by the last house: Good morning, they shout from their terrace. Their huge Great Dane named Ramses barks at me. After that it is silent. I can hear the birds and the rustling leaves. There is the first cornfield! I take my mobile in my hand ready to push the button for the police. Nothing happens and I feel foolish. It goes steeply uphill now, also next to a cornfield. But I am busy keeping up my speed and keeping my breathing down up that hill. Then comes the reward: downhill to the southern edge of the forest. A rabbit jumps out of the bushes and runs – scares me. Then my path goes uphill and through the courtyard of a farm. I have permission to cross. Now I am next to a creek, lots of bushes and at the northern edge of the same forest. I feel semi-safe there, having walked here hundreds of times. Even the last stretch, uphill again, now in the forest, can not frighten me – I thought. I hear a sh sh sh sh! My heart thumps instantly. What is it? Oh, there, it's a bloody crow! Calm down, Isolde, silly. And at the top of the hill I come to the first houses of the village. Josef is outside: Isolde, since when are you wearing a hat? Well, since the summer sun is shining and the corn is so high. Why the corn? he asks. What hat is this anyways? It is a hat from South Africa, I explain. What? Have you been there? No, I bought it in Dubai (at the School Fair). I look fearsome with it, like an American or Canadian cowboy, like a fierce South African, like a stalwart farmer from New Zealand! Get the message? Why don't you go swimming instead, he advises. I have been, Josef. The water was so cold that I would have complained had that been Dubai. But everybody found it to be warm. So I swam half a kilometre. Came through all right, did not shake when I came out. Felt victorious!

Notes from the 48th North

Sent: Thursday, 1 October 2009 ~ 7.35am

It was such beautiful autumn weather that I had my car window down instead of the AC running. I was on my way home from Muehldorf and felt really good driving along, letting my thoughts wander. Yes, I know that I should not do this "while operating a vehicle". And, indeed, I got confused as only a person having lived in all kinds of environments on the globe can be. I drove up to the intersection where I have taken countless left turns before. Trucks in front of me blocked my vision considerably. But I did see camels and lamas in the meadow beyond the left-turn lane. Did not think anything of it. Have seen it before. Those animals do live at the lower Himalayas and in South America, right? And in Dubai! Of course, they are out grazing. I do not know for how many seconds I tried to make sense out of that picture. I did not know where I was! Wait a minute, where am I? Definitely not in one of those places. But where is this? I am in the south of Bavaria, right? Yes, I should stop traveling for I am losing contact with reality! There are indeed those exotic animals here, on a Bavarian meadow, peacefully browsing away. It is reality! The light changed, I had to drive on, crazy or not. The trucks took turns and then I saw the circus tent and all the trailers with it! You had me worried there for a while.

Notes from the 48th North

Sent: Saturday, 26 September 2009 ~ 9.16am

I asked my husband again: You mean we truly go on vacation? No appointments, no quick meeting in between because of a chance opportunity? Yep, he said. Well, I thought, I will be darned and we will see. One early, early morning in September, our long-time taxi driver took us to the Munich airport again. We loaded two heavy suitcases, two carry-ons and, ah, one laptop, onto the airport trolley. Back to Dubai, Mrs. Martin? Ezio asks. No, we fly to California. Please pick us up again on the 15th. Ciao, Ezio.

After an eleven-hour trip just from Frankfurt we came in over the San Francisco Bay. And how long are you going to stay, the customs officer asked me the inevitable question as I stood next to my husband. The rule is the rule. I am fingerprinted and iris-scanned and waved on. My husband can come off a by now fourteen-hour trip since getting up in Munich, renting a car and driving for another two hours to Sacramento. However, it took more than three hours to cover the distance. After all, it was Labor Day weekend and the Oakland Bay Bridge was closed. Repairs had to be done when people did not need to go to work. As a result the Golden Gate Bridge and the San Mateo Bridge were packed with cars. I regretted not being able to come in to see the place where my marriage was registered. We could not swing, as we usually do, through Berkeley, where my husband has to visit his university and Wurster Hall, his College of Environmental Design, remembering the "wild sixties", the student riots, the kite-flying contest, and so forth. Memory lane must be revisited!

In Sacramento we had a barely two-day family reunion. I love those dinners or brunches with all my in-laws. Next morning we visited my mother-in-law at the nursing home. Unlike in May, this time we could not tell if she was aware of her son's visit. But we were prepared for that and accepted that indicator of decline, or perhaps it was just a bad day.

Out in the parking lot of the nursing home was our rental car. Perhaps because of Labor Day the company really did not have another car to offer, other than that fire engine red Chevrolet Camero. It had the appearance of a race car. The back and the front were so high that one couldn't see where the car ends in either direction. Two workers came towards us pushing huge garbage cans. From ten metres away they shouted: What a car, sir! Is this a six-cylinder? My husband looked up, shrugged his shoulders and shouted back: Don't know but it goes bat out of hell! Goodbye then you all. We are off to Napa Valley! With this car? With this car!

Entering the wine-producing area, we felt nostalgic. When we lived in Arizona, back in 1974, and we had little money, we had been here once before. Would you believe it – with a fire engine red car, our VW beetle? And one could not see both ends of that car either! Only this time we did not drive down the winery road, tasting four different wines from almost every winery there was in those days! You see Beringer winery there, should we revisit? I asked. No, my husband said, we have been there. But we have not seen the Geysers, the hot springs of Napa Valley, last time. Let's go, two nature freaks yell. Where to? Calistoga! Oh, wonderful, but why did we not do that last time? Well, the wine and our age perhaps?

In Calistoga we ate at a new historic restaurant. That's what I said – new historic. We could see our car parked at the opposite side of the street. When we came back to drive off to the hot springs, a young girl walked by: That is some car, great car, sir! An elderly man complimented us on our car a few seconds later. I do not like this car, said my husband. It attracts too much attention.

Some time was spent at the hotel pool. Hardly anybody was there. It was so very quiet around us. Napa Valley is peace and serenity. I could hear my nerves fire. Do you hear the Blue Jay? My husband asked in a whisper. Yes, I do! Does he remember my wild Blue Jays in the Santa Monica Mountains that ate out of my hand? Or what is it? A thought formed in my mind. I asked him if he ever felt homesick for Northern California. No, he said firmly.

After four blissful days of following our noses and the healing absence of a ringing mobile we had to pack our bags, head for San Francisco airport, turn in our fire engine race car and head for Oregon, specifically for my husband's place of birth by the mighty Columbia River and between two volcanoes. In Portland we rented another car, a Hyundai, thank you. What should have taken us two hours we stretched into three because we stopped to feast our eyes and our senses on nature's beauty. A waterfall of enormous height cascaded over volcanic rock down into a basin and on down into a second basin where we stood enjoying the cooling mist. There were more of these white water falls to come in this state. They were all awe-inspiring. Throughout our bare four days in Columbia, I was aware of the tremendous change in Hood River Valley from a burning hot desert to a comfortably warm, lusciously green valley.

We visited family history, took a canoe and paddled on Lost Lake, a wilderness park right at the foothills of Mount Hood, the volcano that had dominated the surroundings of my husband's childhood. Now he was walking, driving and paddling on all the familiar territory of his young life until the class of '59 graduated and he left for college. I felt that he was on home turf but not back home. California seemed more home, topped by his adopted home of the Munich area. Nobody would have predicted that in those days.

Few of his classmates had left. Most stayed, so we gathered at the class reunion. The school building no longer existed. Therefore it all happened on top of a hill in the gardens of a golf club. This was a most fitting venue. In front of me I could see Mount Hood with its glaciers shining in the setting sun. Turning the opposite way there was Mount Adams, the twin volcano on the other side of the Columbia River, already in the state of Washington. Secretly I regretted that neither of the two mountains smoked a little, just a little, not more.

Who, the speaker asked, came from more than 5000 miles away? Slowly my husband stood up to his full height. He remained the only one standing. How far? the speaker asked. Halfway around the world, my husband said with a slight tremor in his voice.

A murmur went through the audience. There was one more question the speaker had: And did you come for another reason or just to see us? Just to see you all, my husband answered. It brought down the house.

Goodbye Oregon, you are a wild beauty. Goodbye California, you are a home.

So now we are back in Germany. One day after our arrival my husband left for a day trip to Berlin. Two days after our arrival he left for Saudi Arabia.

There are those who have to travel and there are those who have to hold down the fortress.

Notes from the 48th North

Sent: Saturday, 12 December, 2009 ~ 3.00am

I took my breakfast and placed myself in front of the terrace door to see it snowing. You see, when I was visiting here during Christmas vacation, and coming from all corners of the globe, I did see snow occasionally. But now that I am living here it snows differently, not occasionally. It snows like it did when I was living here as a kid and as a teenager. The TV is running next to me and dribbling alpine music into my ears. Outside, cameras placed in the big ski areas in Tirol and the state of Salzburg and also in the Bavarian Alps, sweep across the mountains. They are reporting one metre of snow, and counting! I catch a severe case of nostalgia. Memories come to the surface of my neo-cortex. Like this one:

It was in the Tennengebirge in the Salzburg area. Ten of us were taking skiing lessons in the hopes of looking a little better and feeling a little more confident on the slopes. You need to go a little into bent knees and lean a little forward. Otherwise it will throw you backwards at the slightest buckel (mogel). So spoken and demonstrated by Adi, our ski instructor, proud wearer of the Land Salzburg Ski Instructors ski jacket. It is my turn to demonstrate that I can follow his instructions. Well, that is okay, I hear him comment on my first swing. The second one gets me off the piste into the deep snow. It slowed me suddenly and I am bent forward by velocity more than I intended to.

Annamirl! Are you looking for mushrooms? he yelled after me.

Notes from the 48th North

Sent: Tuesday, 26 January 2010 ~ 4.15am

It is thawing out, Isolde, spring is around the corner, you can take your Siberian jacket off! So spoke by my next-door neighbor and schoolmate more than a week ago.

But this morning, when I risked my customary first glance out the window after getting up, everything was white again. We got a fresh heavenly supply of snow, about ten centimetres and counting.

I dressed in my Siberian jacket and went to my neighbor for fresh bread rolls and salt for the walkways. He has been shoveling snow, he told me; he is freezing in this Siberian cold. Touch my hands, he said, ice cold, freezing, blue, no blood circulation. Have you ever heard of gloves, Al? Sepp came into the store. I am so cold, he said. I have been shoveling snow. Touch my hands. I can give you a pair of gloves, Sepp. Why would you have some, from Dubai and all? He grinned at me knowingly. I beg your pardon? You guys don't know how to live a winter-adjusted life – I am dressed in several layers and don't freeze. But I do get a lot of sarcasm from y'all. Today I am getting even! Have you adjusted, you keep on asking me. No, but I do remember my childhood. How about you? Two of you are in rehab for winter accidents, a smashed cheek and ear, slipping on ice, and Fritz for turning his tractor over onto its side on snow and ice. Did you hear that the northern and middle German canals are frozen over with twenty-centimetre thick ice? Did you hear that Berlin's highest temp for today is -13C degrees? Yes, we have only -10C at night, still everything is frozen. That's how it used to be when we were kids. Global warming has spoiled us a bit. I tell you what, let's have some fun. Are you all up for a snowball fight come afternoon? Put on goggles so that nobody loses an eye. Isolde, you are crazy, they agree.

I know and I love it.

I did not remind them that in 1996 I had slipped on black ice and broke my upper fema (the bone that connects the upper thigh bone to the pelvis). I felt humble and unfair, but I did defend myself against the teasers, didn't I?

Notes from the 48th North

Sent: Thursday, 28 January 2010 ~ 2.39am

I came back home in the dark of the night. The drive was treacherous. But the village is softly lit up by the orange light of the street lamps. It looks very romantic and softens me too. The wind blows very dry snow through the crisp, if not bitter, cold air. Getting out of the car, my footsteps were deep in powder and disturbed virgin terrain. The car tracks from a few hours before were gone. The snow on the ground around me sparkled vividly as I moved. The wind drove clouds of snow through the air. The flakes glittered briefly as they passed through the light beams. It felt as if I was standing in a diamond shower and lots of them had fallen on the ground. This would be a night for lovers to take a night walk, I thought. Where are they? I only wear these kinds of diamonds because they look best on me. Well then, this is the dream powder for skiers – if they know how to ski on it and don't look for mushrooms instead.

Notes from the 48th North

Sent: Thursday, 18 February 2010 ~ 10.49am

It is over, we did it. The masks have disappeared from the downtown areas. The cowboys, the sheiks, the sailors, the Draculas, the Mexican hats, the Cleopatras, the princesses, the vamps, the hula-hula maidens, the gypsies, the alternate personas, they have gone back into the respective drawers to be revitalized next year. They have done a marvelous job in liberating the inhibited for a few disco nights, ballroom nights, for the crazy days of the Carnival grand finale. It was very cold all along, but that can not stop the masked. It is Germany's fifth season. A couple of Schnapps and you feel fine. And on Ash Wednesday, today, we simply eat salty fish. Till next year, when we can be out of character again. It feels so good, try to stop us!

On the last day, the craziest one of all the Carnival days, it was blue sky and glittering snow and very cold. I took my walk at noon. I met our mayor right in front of the southern forest. Stanislaus, why are you taking pictures of our village? Aren't you supposed to represent the municipality at the Rose Ball in a few hours? No, I am preparing for the citizen assembly on Saturday. No time for Carnival foolishness. Are you coming on Saturday, Isolde? Well, I am afraid so. See you then! I went home and sent him a few of my pictures of the village and surrounding landscape. Isolde, can I use those for "Impressions of Our Village"? Sure, no problem. Here is another one of Al shoveling snow. Defend me if he gets mad at me for taking his picture. That keeps the Carnival going a little longer and the serious, boring stuff off the agenda for a while.

Notes from the 48th North

Sent: Wednesday, 24 February 2010 ~ 11.30am

First I woke up at 1.00am. Had a strange feeling as if I should know something. But no – nothing. Weird, though. Go back to sleep, I told myself. Oh ja, Chris is still playing Xbox with friends in Colorado. Don't you need some sleep before we have to leave for the airport at the crack of dawn? Useless, I know. Well, I will drive then, because I have had the most sleep. There will be no ice on the roads, they said. At 2.00am I woke up with a jolt. This time I know there is a rumbling noise and quite loud. Son is asleep. No light under his door anymore. What is that? Not normal! I will have to find the source if I want to sleep again. I keep very still, can't hear a thing. Sounds like somebody or some animal is on the roof or, worse, in the attic. Or is it downstairs? I take that huge flashlight, go onto the balcony first, check out the yard from up there. Nothing! Very cold barefoot on the balcony in February. Well, I have been subject to paranoia before. Does not touch me anymore. I go back to bed, take a book to read until my thumping heart calms down. But just as I got into the story there is another strong rumbling noise. Came from the roof, I swear. It is not my imagination. But did not match what my brain says: earthquake, tornado. No nocturnal animal that ever resided in the attic for the winter can make such a racket. Perhaps a raccoon, I have had a raccoon in the attic in Los Angeles. Somebody is loosening the tiles and letting them slide down. Flashlight, up to the attic, almost as cold as the balcony. Shine the beam into every corner there is and more. Zip! Cannot be an animal. What to do? Again I stand still. And finally I heard the trickle that I should have heard already out on the balcony. Snow is melting – we had Foenwind. That one comes from Italy and North Africa and keeps the night temperature above freezing. The north side of the roof has had a lot of snow on it still and is now sliding down, patch by patch.

Die Moral von der Geschicht: when you are gone for so long, lived in the deserts of the world and the snow-deprived regions, you do not remember all the sounds of your home anymore. All my expat friends, I wonder if they remember all the sounds of their original homes.

Notes from the 48th North

Sent: Friday, 15 February 2010

Again, blue skies and sunshine lit up the piste. The snow is like silk today – so determined by my steadfast skiing buddy. But an hour later it had softened, was pushed up and carved by other skiers and snowboarders. It took a lot of strong leg muscles to negotiate my way downhill. The next two days I felt those said muscles when climbing or descending stairs and similar movements. That gave me a good excuse to occupy one of those armchairs on the deck of the restaurant building. Well, I did go for a fast walk over slippery packed snow. And then it was time to pack up and head home, a roughly three-hour drive. Even my son did not complain to call it quits – I was skiing my ass off today, he informed us.

You son of a gun, at the age of twenty-four we also did that. But we did not leave our skis stuck in the snow at the parking lot, right in front of the car. We did not have to call back from Bavaria to Tirol to ask the store clerkto save our skis until we come back, the day after tomorrow, to fetch them. What would father Freud say to that?

The next day, what with first taking your father to the Munich airport at the crack of dawn, and then making the round trip driving from there back to the ski area in Austria, you put in an eight-hour day on the steering wheel. Bet you won't forget your skis in the parking lot in Tirol again! But you did secure yourself your desired job in Berlin while hauling ass down the Autobahn (or was it coming down the curved mountain road on the way back home?). That is quite a trick, to speak like a good friend of mine when he is a bit annoyed.

But all is well that ends well. That was the end of the skiing season for this winter then. You, my son, were the fastest of your own

Notes from the 48th North

Olympic season, and you, my husband, were the most elegant skier. I at least tried not to crash in the snow and to make a good figure skiing downhill.

Notes from the 22nd North

Sent: Monday, 15 March 2010 ~ 2.08am

Expats rarely revisit; they are busy with their new challenge in yet another far away land. So I was looking forward to my trial of a revisit in Dubai with a lot of curiosity and apprehension. It was not by accident that I arrived on a Friday morning to join the anniversary of the RL's at the Golf Club. The president of my former RL group was almost adamant about my appearance. I would meet friend and foe all at once. Perhaps I had not been gone long enough, but the welcome was complete. Isolde, you are here! Isolde, did you come back? No way, expats move forward and rarely backwards. Isolde, we missed you. It was like coming home! My id, ego and superego received all the genuine warmth with a matter of course, a matter of affection and a matter of pride. Yes, it felt really good. But all the while I was aware that there was a lot of the element of surprise about my visit mixing with the enthusiastic welcome. When are you coming again? You owe us a reading from your book. Okay, I will come next year perhaps to do this. Next year?! – No, in about six months, we don't care whether it is already out on the market or not. I seemed to hear frustration, after all, they have been asking for that reading for about two years now. They did not forget! In a year, they said, we might not be here anymore. Right, I actually forgot my own credo: expats move on. I will do what I can to keep my promise. Thank you, my friends, you were great.

I'll send you a few pictures. Is it not said that they speak louder than words?

Notes from the 5th North

Sent: Wednesday, 17 March 2010 ~ 1.02am

Every evening a delightfully illustrated Din A5 card is leaning against the pillows. It is the Landaa Reef News written by Kaku, the hermit crab. It is telling what happened under the surface, at the surface and even above the ocean surface. Territorial fights, marriages, hunting expeditions and social gatherings are being reported. Kaku writes in a very engaging style, informs about things marine that I did not know. I decide to find Kaku to thank and compliment it. Should I look for a male or a female? I go to reception and ask to speak to Kaku. I get a blank stare and then a big grin. No Ma'am, we are not writing this. Perhaps you should go to the marine research centre. Oh, thank you, I have been there in their lab yesterday and received a nice welcome into their holy halls. Hi there again, Isolde, you came back? Yes, may I speak to Kaku, the hermit crab? Yes, you are speaking to her. Linda, the marine biologist, smiles from ear to ear. What a nice idea, Linda, may I request to be friends on Facebook? Oh, yes, and use my email, I will send you all back issues from Kaku. I have done this for six months now. Thank you, I am so glad I met you, don't know when or where I might meet you again. I sure do enjoy short stories. I wonder where that sudden interest came from?

Spotlight on a Stream of Consciousness

Notes from the 48th North

Sent: Sunday, 2 May 2010 ~ 12.14am

I was just waking up, but kept very still to listen to the calling of the cuckoo. How nice a sound, one that I have always loved but not heard too often due to my absences. It sounded so clear, like it came from a well-tuned piano. Bloody early though for the bird. It was just barely dawning. And the sound was also so regular and persistent. This is something else, I thought. Yes, it was the alarm clock from the mobile of my son in the next room. Oh, yes, he and his Dad have to drive 600km to Berlin today. Son has finally found his own place and is moving his stuff from Bavaria to Prussia. Need to get up, fix a breakfast American-redneck style. It will be a long haul. But today is Sunday, should be okay traffic. Good thing they stayed out of Berlin on the first of May, Labor Day. Each year everybody is out to protest something. 6,000 determined-looking police were in waiting! But today it should be fine when they reach the city around noon. But before you go could you please plug the extension cord back in? My phone is dead, and my salt lamp and my protection against flashes of lightening hitting and burning up my computer system as well. Take another one. Do you still have my bank card? Where? On your bedside table, are you sure? We were outside packing the car to the hilt. But it was a pleasant morning (without cuckoo calling). A soft rain was making gentle, calming, reassuring sounds as the drops hit the leaves. It was a typical May rain. The air felt so clean and soft. It should be a pleasant drive with my son driving in the middle lane, and Daddy, the navigator, surely sleeping in the passenger seat. You are saying you should be back tonight at about 10.00pm? Lo and behold! Could you at least stop when you enter the Bohemian Forest National Park and look at the bears and wolves for a while, sleep a little, and then go on? See you, Inshallah, as we used to say back in Dubai.

Notes from the 32nd North

Sent: Tuesday, 25 May 2010 ~ 8.28am

We have been invited for an evening meal at the Purple Moon, downtown Beirut. Met at 10.00pm at the restaurant. The streets were very narrow, stop-and-go traffic with pedestrians, motorcycles and bikes crisscrossing in every direction, like it only can be in an Arab city. Since it was much more stop than go the taxi driver started a conversation with the inevitable question: Where are you from? I tried to distract him: *Ana minh Almanya*. Oh, Germany! I love German soccer. I favour your team for the championship. Very good, thanks, but where is the Purple Moon? Right here, enjoy your meal.

It is a narrow room but long. Most tables had one or two people sitting there. So few people, does it tell me something about the food? We ordered, got our beverages served, etc. It is 11.00pm now, and food has not yet arrived but more and more patrons appeared. They were of all ages and shapes. Now there were no more free seats to be had. Live music started. We had to shout at each other now. The place went up in cigarette smoke. That, and trying to talk, my throat and my voice did not take kindly to. Food arrived. We ate in silence. The music and the singing still got louder. The volume seemed to vibrate in my chest. It was the same sensation when the first commercial jets were thundering over me at the end of the runway in Munich (those were the days when people could still come up to the fence of an airfield and watch planes coming and going). We gave up communicating and instead wrote messages on paper napkins. But then that stopped as well, because the patrons had begun to sing along. Some were standing in the aisles. Some had started to dance right there. By 1.00am I stood there as well, trying to dance a Sirtaki in a Lebanese night club in Beirut. People still kept coming. Most never sat down but sang and danced with a drink in one hand. And suddenly I remembered that I had to be on a plane the next day and still needed to pack. We had used up most of the paper napkins. But I needed one more. I need to leave, have to pack, have to sleep and don't want to get sick on the plane. I showed it to our host. He wrote back: *They will be shocked. Nobody leaves before 4.00am! Sorry, so sorry, have mercy, I need to go.* So we left. Outside the door, on the sidewalk, something seemed wrong. It was so eerily quiet, like it usually is when it snows at night. But that was not the case. I asked host, hostess and husband: Do you hear this muffled silence? Yes, host and hostess said. Your hearing will have recovered in about thirty minutes. I asked my husband: Are your ears functioning normally? He answered: Huh?

Notes from the 48th North

Sent: Tuesday, 1 Jun 2010 ~ 3.02am

Pretty soon I will be homesick for Dubai, the desert, 40C degrees, summer clothes. Beats 14C degrees as summer temperature, doesn't it? I had forgotten what three weeks of rain can be like. Well, they can mean water puddles, cars splashing at pedestrians, umbrellas getting tangled up with other umbrellas, cafe house visits to talk to the nice guy who's umbrella ran into yours. Yes, rain is a tool to socialise. Singing in the rain ... but what about my power walks? I am happy to get sopping wet when it is a warm summer rain, but this three-week encounter is for the birds. Speaking of birds ... I decided to get on the stationary bike and the rowing machine in a boring room. Bad because the activity is boring already. But try me. I opened the window wide, put the equipment smack in front of it, and there I go. The rain looked like strings coming down from a gray sky. The drops made a nice, regular clicking sound. The wish-wush of the leaves of the nut tree added to the rain day symphony. It was an enjoyable, calming, comforting sound mix that gave rise to a pleasant feeling. The air felt fresh but no longer cold. A number of different species of birds were hopping around in the grass, picking up something and flying off into trees and under the roof of the barn only to be back promptly. The sparrow is attacking the starling, the bachstelze with its long legs is oblivious to the fight. But this one with the red underside of its tail is pursuing another unknown bird. No racism there. How long have I been on the bike now? Geez, much too long, I could have stopped fifteen minutes ago.

Notes from the 48th North

Sent: Thursday, 10 June 2010 ~ 8.41am

Even if one is not a soccer fan by any stretch of the imagination, one cannot escape the hype that has been building since I came back from Beirut some three weeks ago. They, the Lebanese, had their cars, motorbikes or bikes decorated with at least one flag (square that at least) to signal favoritism and to invite betting, the greatest fun of all. So coming back home I was already tuned in a bit. I did see a few cars with our flag on the roof or sticking out the window at my return. But that was then. Tomorrow is the first day of the next four weeks. When I was in my gardening store to get a pair of scissors and saw the boxes of flags in all sizes, I knew I was in for more to come. Today I am trying to protect my car from flagpoles scratching my fender and from drivers drunk with anticipation. All the public viewing places have gigantic screens sparkling in the sun in any bigger city. In 2006 those places and streets had as many shouting, loving, singing, dancing, drinking people congregated that would fit and some more. Everybody hugged and kissed everybody. There were no more barriers between race, gender, religion, poor, not so poor, nationalities, left and right, etc. It was one grand party all over Germany. I was so moved when our players at the end came back to Berlin wearing T-shirts saying *Danke*. And the fans carried banners that read, *Ihr seid die Weltmeister der Herzen* – You are the champions of our hearts. But get the significance of this: these were all the nationalities cheering the third-place German team. A reporter asked Turkish people, whose team did not get anywhere, about that. Well, we are Germans as well, we live here! they said. I remember what the Kaiser said: *So stellt sich der liebe Gott die Welt vor* – that's how God imagines his world to be! I think we are in for it again. Anderl decorated his disco-soccer-cottage with flags, the black red and gold one. He turns on his charm when he asks me if I would get upset when they get a bit louder as usual or scream even. No, go ahead, if you still scream at 4.00am. I will come and join you. And if you are unusually quiet I will also come and invite you for a group session to take you through the first stage of the mourning process.

The soccer fever, we got it good! This is *Ausnahmezustand* – a state of emergency – as we have had before. We and the rest of Europe go nuts over the world championships. But then it is good for the balance of our souls to go nuts every once in a while. Do I care who will be the new champion? Some. But my absolute favorite final would be Germany against the USA, then I will cheer on both teams!

Notes from the 48th North

Sent: Tuesday, 15 June 2010 ~ 5.48pm

I love that two-minute walk to the village store at 8.00am to get freshly-baked bread for breakfast. Elli put the basket in front of me. Which ones would you like, Isolde? Albert came in smoking his breakfast pipe. Will be smoked bread today, I thought. Good morning, Isolde, he shouted. Listen up, I was in Munich yesterday and saw a book of yours in the bookstore, he said with a grin. Since when do you go to browse in bookstores? I wanted to ask boldly. But I was so stunned that I actually looked at him, saying nothing. What? How does he know about my book? Albert, get off my case! Ah, if I am telling you! You are pulling my leg, Albert, get off! Then he described the cover, and it was correct. I was puzzled. He certainly reads newspapers but probably not books per se. Moreover, my book was definitely not in local bookstores. Since I was not to be fooled he gave up. No, I was at Anton's place. I saw it there. But I could not read anything, only your name. It was all in English! Why did you write that book in English? We can't read it! Why did you not write it in German? We are here, you are here in Germany and you are one of us! Listen to this! The last statement – You are one of us! I smiled diplomatically and let him spend his words. I did not have the heart to tell him that my definition of "us" has changed and I do not feel that much "us" anymore, not for quite a number of years. But I think I heard a compliment within the accusations.

Notes from the 48th North

Sent: Friday, 25 June 2010 ~ 7.20pm

Before I go downtown to the supermarket I have to go to Fred to bring him the plans. Servus, Isolde, come in, let's take a quick look. Before we open the drawings he asks: Where is Steve? Not here, no. I give Fred his email address and phone number. Thank you very much, I have to run, want to get my grocery shopping behind me before the big crowd hits. Although that big crowd is also the reason that I meet friends and neighbors there in that store. Usually results in a nice chat.

This time I meet my recently retired GP and his wife. A big smile. How are you? Have you adjusted to my successor, he asks. Where is your husband? In Beirut? Tell him to be careful, not to work so much. How often do you two meet? He is all concerned about our mental and physical health. Now it is my turn to warn you, dear doc. How is your book doing on the market? Oh it is there, he says, I am traveling a lot to give presentations – sometimes four hours at a lick. Knowing that he has taken beta blockers for twenty years I ask: You can stand in one place for that long? Remember when you told me to walk back and forth when I do presentations? Good luck, see you around. Have to go because at 1.00pm, KK comes with his tractor and wagon.

Albert is going to use it as a platform to cut his wild growing hedge into our garden. Eventually I join them. When is Steve coming again, Albert asks. Here comes his son. Albert has cut the electrical cord. Son is taking over. Where is Steve, he asks. I have an idea, in future, every time he is here I will hang out the California flag. And nobody needs to ask me again. This is only partially concern about my mental state. This is watching me. I know you guys well. Sepp told me a lot the other day when he joked: Make sure you don't email too many good looking men, Isolde. I am an adult, you guys, I do as I please! I know I should appreciate their concern about my mental well-being. But then there is that "watch-her-morals" feeling I sense.

Nope, no paranoia but amusement. They are my folks from my childhood.

Notes from the 48th North

Sent: Friday, 25 June 2010 ~ 8.08pm

I thought this would leave me cooler, would omit this subject, but it is just too interesting to stay cool: The state of the sixth season in German: The soccer WM (Weltmeisterschaft), of course. Is anything else happening in the world? The results and how they were derived is breaking news, frontrunner to politics and the oil spill in the Gulf of Mexico. When I was out gardening and tidying up in front of the house the school bus arrived. The girls and boys that poured out had the flag painted on their faces. They were in school like that! A few minutes later Mart stops his car sharply two millimetres from my toes, jumps out and hugs me for a mere card and taking pictures of his tin can littered garden, a thing done here when a baby has been born. Well, tell me about it, how is your wife and your little brand new Lena? He is one happy first time father. But here comes the important stuff: Soccer tonight, Germany against Cameroon. I will come later, he says, going to the hospital first. And then he will join his friends and watch the soccer game. Must admit I am wavering between understanding and not. If you don't feel like watching it, he says, you don't have to because when we score a goal you will hear it, and when they score you will hear the difference. Well, I watched it. At 3.00am that night I was awake again and heard the last cars drive home from the semi-public viewing place at Anderl's. Thank you guys for letting me sleep after the ordeal! And we will do the same again on Sunday, the classic foe England, seven times they have played against each other in the quarter finals, semi-finals and finals. Who could stay away from it? You can't, I hear over the phone from Beirut. When we lived in LA we had to buy a rinky-dink TV set so that you could watch the championships – in Spanish! So my love reminds me! (The US knew nothing about soccer in those days.) It is true, I did not understand a word but I could see enough. One Spanish word I still remember: Coppa del Mundo. I fear Germany will lose against the English on Sunday. Then we can relax again.

The clothing industry has put a T-shirt on the market that will turn orange when the wearer gets excited. So if the Dutch should have to play Germany I will try to find victims. It is the fun that counts, isn't it?

Notes from the 48th North - The Classic Game?

Sent: Sunday, 27 June 2010 ~ 10.53am

Did you watch that soccer match? It was one of the finest. I do not mean who won or lost, no I mean the two wonderfully sovereign teams. It was conducted with so much fairness in the absence of rude, injuring fouls. My respects to the English team since they had more reason to lose their cool. But they did not! Only one yellow card was passed out in the whole game! If you consider that this was a knockout game, an all-or-nothing matter, they were to be admired. I saw fans from both teams sitting together, waving their different flags in unison and in friendship. So far there were no ugly happenings after the game. In Berlin 300,000 people came to the "fan mile" to watch the match together on a gigantic screen. It was reported that strangers hugged each other and shared food and drinks. Proves that not only pain wants to be a shared experience. It was one big party there, and not only there. That's the way to go. There is one issue, though, where I beg to differ: as a kid I was taught that sports has nothing to do with politics. Well, at the G20 summit in Canada there was a break just for this soccer match. In the first row of viewers sat the German chancellor and the British premier! Wonder whether the psychology carried over to their further meetings?

Well, let me tell you then where Steve is. He is in Beirut. At 3.00pm, I read an email from him saying he is going to a big society wedding tonight. For that he has to drive to Biblos, the ancient city by the coast, the one that I did not see when I was in Lebanon in May. Lucky you! At 6.00pm he calls me from inside the church, after the wedding, so that I can hear Arab Christian church music. At 8.00pm he calls me from the hotel where the reception is taking place. Are there a lot of screeching birds around? Screeching birds? he asks. No, it sounds like screeching to you over the phone but it is a frog in the pond on the hotel terrace. Have you separated from the wedding party then? Any dinner yet? No, but I will have to wait for it before I drive back, he says. Well, then when you are back have a good night's sleep. No, he says, I will go straight back to the construction site. We are going to pour concrete all night. Are you telling me you will go in your suit and Gucci shoes to watch pouring concrete? Perhaps with a pretty white helmet on your cotton pickin' head? Yes, he says. Oh please, send me a picture! And anybody watch the milestone soccer game there?

Notes from the 48th North

Sent: Sunday, 20 June 2010 ~ 10.30am

Sunday, 4.30am – alarm clock going off with a gentle melody. Get up, shower, get dressed, grab a cup of tea, get into the car and drive to the airport – routine. Do you have your passport, e-ticket, mobile? No, don't have mobile, turn round, get mobile, go to the airport. Will take a little longer due to the little lakes on an uneven road. Look at this field, a big lake, look at those Scottish Highlands cows, they are laying down in the sopping wet, almost flooded meadow – tough guys! Water, water every where, a blind man can see. A jogger runs by on the bicycle path splashing along. I will have to do my power-walk in rubber boots today. That, in turn, causes me to have a flashback – theatre at CAC in Cairo. The theatre and drama group perform the rubber boot dance. Very rhythmic stepping of about fifty students on stage, don't think there was any music with it. Stomping their feet in rubber boots was the way workers in African mines communicated with each other as they were not allowed any other form of communication between them; so it says in the flyer. I could choreograph a spectacular rubber boot dance in flooded streets here. It would look really good with water splashing up around us. Would that not be the answer to relentless rain and seasonal depression? We are not going to be subdued by mere rain! Yes, that is effective coping. Beats the hell out of wishing to return to the deserts of the world!

Notes from the 48th North

Sent: Wednesday, 30 June 2010 ~ 6.46pm

I am getting married on Saturday 1.00pm, he said. Here in our church? Yep, are you coming to church? Of course, I will come! I would not miss this for anything. He looked at me with suspicion. Well, because you are you and I will hang out the flag for you, too. Why? More suspicion. Because it is reason to celebrate, you are our Maxl and the soft sides in you deserve it. I hung it out for Willi when he got married. Okay, he said, I will look for it.

Uschi and I re-entered the village coming back from our walk. She carried her dog with the hip problem. Out of breath and with a flick of her head she pointed at his house. His friends are all lamenting about his wedding date, she said. What's wrong with it? They can't watch the soccer game!

We met Mart, also a member of the steadfast-every-Monday-every-game-soccer-disco club. He joined us in our conversation. We have asked the restaurant for a TV, he said. Thankfully, this relationship has already been going for a few years. The wedding is only a sort of finalisation act, I thought. Yesterday at 9.00pm a couple came into our yard asking if they could put up the scaffolding for the wedding party in here. The ground is even and there are these rose bushes in the background, so the photographer pleaded.

Of course you can. But I have to be able to drive out of here, need to go to the airport. When? At 2.30. Oh, by that time we are long gone. We all want to watch the soccer game. Are you not going to watch it? I can't, I have to pick somebody up at the airport. Time for the kick-off and the plane landing are the same, 4.00pm. Oh, shit, he said to that.

Why don't you go into the Bavarian beer garden at the airport and watch it there, Albert was suggesting. He always gives me free advice. What is more important, Steven or the soccer game? Albert! Besides, has it come down to that? I think there are two more weeks of this.

Notes from the 48th North

Sent: Monday, 12 July 2010 ~ 6.33am

Why the reservations? My son asked. No, we don't come to check up on you, we merely want to see you. So I reassure him. Nothing could be a more sincere answer than that. But it is also true that father and son have been on my case to show me Berlin. And if I think about it, a lot of other people have looked at me with disbelief when they found out I have seen so many capitals around the globe excluding my own. So it was high time to go there. What they all don't know, but some have guessed, is that I needed to go somewhere. A habit of decades has ingrained in my brain that signal "time to pack again". And I did pack for a three-day trip with the same mindset of a four-week trip. When I also took all my liquids and put them into this sealed plastic bag to be presented to the airport security I finally caught myself. Hey, Isolde, you will be driving, not flying, you will not cross international borders. It is easy! After that, I was packed in no time flat. Didn't even bother to make a decision about doubtful items to take or not to take. Just throw it into the trunk of the car. Basta!

I drove the first half of the 600kms. To approach Berlin and then find our hotel I cowardly left to my husband. But then I became the VIP unexpectedly as I could understand the local tongue. The route we had selected beforehand was all blocked off. We took left turns and right turns until we were on a small road that had no name and was not on the map. Nonetheless (you should have bought a Navi!) we sat in the car, windows down, each one studying a map. A heavy man walked by pushing a wheelbarrow and smiled at me, walking on. Then he came back and asked in heavy Berlin slang to help. Yep, I did understand him. The first friendly Prussian face. His directions were such that I could follow them. Good start.

After I had recuperated from the path-finding in a cool hotel and when the sun started to lose some of its power I was ready to go out on that most famous of all streets in Berlin, the one praised by so many songs ("I am homesick for Kurfuerstendamm, Berlin hassle and bustle and tamtam ..."). I took a stroll, tried to get a feel for the atmosphere, could not decide whether I was a foreigner or a native, felt good about what I saw, and ambivalent about how I belonged or not. Great place, lots of life's "tamtam" going on. Charming, friendly faces during rush hour! I am glad I came. Look at that church – the Kaiser-Wilhelm-Gedäechtniskirche – without a steeple, without a body, without bells, black from fire long ago. WWII sent a shocking reminder. An intentionally very modern steeple held up the bells high, sounding crystal clear into the evening. These two have been there, parallel, for a few decades and will be there into the future. The burned-out steeple-less, bodiless ruin will never be torn down. So decided by the City of Berlin, also long ago. I shuddered at the most recent history of this centuries-old city. Guess I am home right now.

CM and his roommate, an almost native Berliner, took us through town, starting early on Saturday morning when the city was gradually coming to life. This is the Reichstag, the Parliament, the Chancellery, the embassies, the river. We were crisscrossing, took the underground, rested in a street cafe in front of a Barock building out of Prussian history. What is it? Our son's roommate knew it all. A terrific tour guide he was (on a Saturday morning when he could have slept in). Husband needed to find his building completed about ten years ago, son needed an ATM machine. There, the roommate points with his finger at Potsdamer Platz, is an exhibition of Salvatore Dali's artwork. I knew he wanted to see it and so did I. An unexpected treat. No, I do not have to see Check Point Charley. I have already seen a piece of The Wall. Let's go to the Dali exhibition. Who knows when I will run into one of those again?

And this, this is the fan mile. You mean this is where the 100,000 fans watch the soccer games? Ja! Looks very barren and smaller than on TV without the masses of screeching people. Let's be gone from here in another hour or so. Today, Germany is playing against Spain! Serious, that is, yes.

You were a great guide, roommate. *Danke vielmals*! And you, my son, are a joy, you have made a nice place for yourself. I can see why we need to come here and not vice versa. Okay then, see you all when the Oktoberfest is on in Munich. We will make a place for all of you. I can't wait!

Tonight, though, I will have a date with Prussian history. But first we had to get to the Charlottenburg Castle which was built, or at least started, in 1701. The dinner served in there will be consisting of dishes that King Friedrich I liked. The ceremonial master and everybody else being any kind of servant tonight had been put into historical clothing and employed historical behaviour, a special treat, a theatre. I was necessarily in it. You are of the most exquisite beauty at the eleventh hour, the ceremonial master spoke. Fun to dive into history, times gone by, like this one. But the concert of baroque music, even the Brandenburg Concerto from Bach, was trying my ears.

It was time to leave. My mind has been pacified until the travel bug calls on me again. Where are you going? The hotel checkout lady asked. I heard myself and my husband answer in unison: Home. Where is that, she inquired. Munich, we said. That sounded right. And now, I have seen my capital. I can identify with it, within limits. After all, I am Bavarian, not Prussian. In the winter it will be worth another visit, backstage Berlin.

Notes from the 48th North

Sent: Monday, 26 July 2010 ~ 1.24am

I have deliberately omitted this from my book – the subject of expat love affairs. It would be too hot a subject matter for some countries. But the issue has not left my mind as I am still confronted, touched, drawn into it.

What should I do, Isolde, what do you think? Well, I think you should not have a love affair in Arabia. Given the right circumstances it is illegal and can carry a prison term. So if you can't help it, get out of here! How good you are moving back to Europe anyway this summer! I bet this will be a conflict, or a goodbye? A few months later she told me with almost penetrating eyes: Isolde, he came to Europe, it is not all over for us! Still, I said, no, I will not be your alibi, it is not included. And then what? He goes back to Arabia and you will visit him there? In six weeks I will go and visit my friends in Arabia! You are disregarding my warnings, young lady, this love has definitely made you blind to danger. Don't be stupid, the world is big, find another place to meet. Well, not this time, but after that it is his turn again to travel – coming to Europe. Really? I hope the two of you have a lot of credit points from the airline. Isolde, we are going to be transfered to Hong Kong! In two months we are leaving. By golly, that will be so much further away and apart. Yep, now what? In June he is coming to Hong Kong. Well, lucky you, he really loves you and you are in a safer place for that kind of thing. Has he won in the lottery? No, but his work takes him traveling – no problem. In the summer I will be home in Europe. Then we are going to meet there again and see you as well. By all means do! And then, before I go back to Hong Kong I have to make a family visit in the Balkans. He will come there for just a short week. And then Back to Hong Kong and then? Don't know. Where there is a will there is a way. Right! If you ever should get married, let me know. I will invite myself to wherever it may be on the globe. This wedding would be a miracle.

I have two more friends who carried on a nomadic expat courtship. It is complicated to be sure, but not crazy. It's enduring love, enduring and hoping! Yep, that it is – twice over.

Date: Thursday, 29 July 2010 ~ 3.37am

MSF, what about our expat love affair? It has been decades, traveled all over the world, gone through good times and not so good times, produced an international love-child and still going strong ... DSM. Yep, my love, we are an expat couple all right. But then we were traveling and moving together, not separate. There was a will, and there was a way. No regrets whatsoever – it was glorious, and still going!

Notes from the 48th North

Sent: Thursday, 29 July 2010 ~ 5.21am

Have been thinking the same thoughts. It is worth another book! Should we?

I am blessed with a great, innovative, creative editor! Was it an accident of chance or predetermined (as Freud might think) that I ran into him?

Spotlight on a stream of consciousness, he called these Notes.

I had never thought about them in terms of their origins in my mind. But his six words enlightened me. He is so right, so precise, so poetic. Now, how does the spotlight fall on one issue and not on another?

Notes from the 48th North

Sent: Friday, 6 August 2010 ~ 12.04pm

This must be the wettest, nastiest, damnedest twenty-four hour day that I have experienced here since the Bohemian Forest has been cut down and regrown. It is not "singing in the summer rain" anymore, it is dashing through the downpour, navigating a car through little lakes, watching the river rise and flood, staying indoors. I was determined not to be a sissy and go walking today. But when the wind drove the rain into my face and whipped my hair around I finally retreated. I got myself busy indoors, had a good time, felt good about my accomplishments. Even went to the municipality for much-needed info. But secretly I had been hoping for a dry evening. Instead it went on just like it did yesterday night and this morning. I started to lose my composure. Called Conrad. His roommate was on the phone. Oh, hello, how are you? he asked. Fine, I answered. No, actually I am not fine anymore, I had enough of this rain. Oh, roommate says, it will pass, has been a bit much, yeah, but see, Conrad is even jogging. He does not mind. How nice of this young guy to try to comfort me verbally. But I am getting homesick. What? Homesick, homesick for the desert, for Dubai, I want 45C degrees. Every day sunshine, heat and sand storms, the beauty and the reliability of the blue desert sky.

What are we going to do with this rainy evening? Grab the Cognac bottle, call up Andy and tell him we are coming. No, do you want to play a game of chess? With you? You have beat me the last three times! Well, grab the bottle of Cognac, drink some and then you can win. No, that is too hot for me. Do you want the Ramazzotti from Italy? The what? The Ramazzotti! What is it? It is like Campari! *Alora*, I will take that if it is safe to drink, then I will beat you. It will put me into the Italy – vacation-in-Finale-Ligure mood. Remember Umberto? The sun, the sand, the sound of the Italian language, the eternally flirting Italians, the beach ball game with a bunch of Italian kids, who could not talk a word to each other but had so much fun. Italy, *sole, amore, baci e vino*. Is it still raining? Yes! Well, I don't care! I am traveling in my mind.

Notes from the 48th North

Sent: Monday, 9 August 2010 ~ 11.39am

This is for my Anglo-Saxon friends and those that eventually came to feel like one ...

Another Anglo-Saxon friend of mine said so on Facebook: Today, in the Anglo-Saxon world at least, the date is 8.9.10. This formation of a date, so he says, is only possible twelve times in a century. And he must know, a master of numbers and a master of chess. See, those are the wits of Anglo-Saxons that got me hooked to you Anglo-Saxons a long time ago. And still collecting friends such as Anton and Cerry ... but then they are Scots, so are they Anglo-Saxons as well?

Notes from the 48th North

Sent: Thursday, 12 August 2010 ~ 8.19pm

Each of the last three years I was aware that between the 10th and the 14th of August the Earth crosses the "dust tail" of a comet. Each summer I was ready to spend a few hours a night of said dates outdoors to watch that meteorite shower thrown by the comet. Each of the three summers those nights had overcast and rainy skies to block the view. So next summer I intend to be south of the Alps stargazing on one of Italy's beaches. *Basta*!

Also each summer I had a favourite summer read. Nothing blocked that view. I read that in my hammock between two apple trees. Next year I hope I'll read in Italy on the beach, even if there should be overcast skies to show what I care if the heavenly spectacle is still not visible to me!

So here is part of this summer's read provided by an unexpected source, my *Prevention* Magazine. Title: Double your Pleasure – It's good for your health.

"Pleasure Principle 1: Indulge in Fun Foods, a) Savor a square of dark chocolate with your cappuccino. The confection boosts blood vessel function by a whopping 129%. b) Sip sangria. More than just a sensational summer cooler, sangria boosts cardiovascular health, thanks to the resveratrol [what is that?] in red wine, plus antioxidants from added fruits and juices."

"Pleasure Principle 2: Schedule Play Dates [& Mental Health Breaks]," It says: Take a guiltless siesta, savour a stroll, the usual relaxation methods.

"Pleasure Principle 3: Stay Intimately Connected, a) Get a little frisky between the sheets. Perhaps the sexiest health news ever: regular orgasms provide remarkable physical benefits. People who have more frequent sex have a) lower blood pressure, half the risk of fatal heart attacks, sounder sleep, less pain, and better immunity, and b) spend the weekend hanging out with your partner. According to a just published study in the Journal of Social and Clinical Psychology, people who spent Friday evenings to Sunday afternoon leisurely with loved ones experienced better moods, greater vitality, and fewer aches and pains."

I think almost all of those exercises in health can be taken to an Italian beach for meteorite shower gazing. So I will just have to see to it that this is not just wishful thinking.

Notes from the 48th North

Sent: Saturday, 21 August 2010 ~ 1.35am

We are going to have three whole days of summer this weekend. So what am I doing indoors? I have a story going around in my head that needs to be written down.

I was sitting in his consulting room in the hospital waiting for the results of my bone scan and mammo, reading a high gloss gossip magazine. He came out in those croc shoes, silently, I did not hear him enter the room. When I looked up I saw an unknown doctor before me, smiling as if we had met before. Hi there, luck is walking on silent soles, Goethe said. You are not Dr. H! Yes, I am Frau Martin! But, doctor, I saw you last time two years ago. You don't look the same!? Remember when I tell you that we had an interesting talk about the SD of my bone density score? He grinned even more. Yes, I know doc, you have seen a few thousand patients since then. Sorry I did not recognize you. Why do you look so different? Maybe, he said, because I let my hair grow long? I loved his straight face and his mischievously sparkling eyes. Indeed! His hair reached down in the back and hung into his forehead to almost eye level. Good thing he is not a surgeon. A penny if you tell me your reason, doc! Well, because I wanted beautiful women look at me again. Did it work? Not too much. Well, doctor, perhaps those women you want to attract go for the personality and combed hair together and in that order. Be brave, your personality would qualify.

So now what? You mean I cannot go skiing anymore? You can, Frau Martin, just do not fall. Doctor, are you a skier? And I just could hear him say: No, I don't do such dangerous sports. I go hang gliding instead. But he smiled – mischievously.

Notes from the 48th North

Sent: Sunday, 22 August 2010 ~ 8.58am

This is the most gorgeous summer morning of what is going to be one of the last lazy, hazy days of summer for this season. None of my three walking buddies are coming along. Suit yourself, your loss, I am off. Hat, sun lotion, sunglasses, camera, mobile, drink, not necessarily in this order. The air feels wonderful, it is liberating, light, gentle, stimulating. Where is Ramses? He is ditching even the morning warmth as if it were heat.

Okay now, I am walking between these two bloody corn fields. Puts me a tunnel and gives me a creepy feeling. Have read reports of bad guys jumping out of those cornfields into the path of single women, too many times for sure. But I have some protection. Pull out my mobile and phone my husband as we agreed I should do. The corn stalks are higher than me. Perhaps they are the reason that it says: Out of coverage area.

Well, speed up, jog and try it again further down. Still does not work – perhaps up on top of the hill. That is the end of the second cornfield, try it, because the next one is down the other slope.

Yes, he answers, how are you so early in the morning?

He is on the phone, it worked. I am walking through the cornfield canyons.

Do you have time to talk to me until I am passed these? Of course I have time for you. Good, thanks, where are you? Oh, it is a hard life today, he says. Are you sure you have time then? Of course, for you I make time. What are you doing, I ask puzzled. Oh, I am out by the pool in a lounge chair trying to read that German magazine.

But the language is so damned difficult. That kind of hard work you mean, well, wish I was there to help. I do too, Liebling. You look so good in your bathing suit. Hold on, I am entering the forest and you are fading away. Call me when I am home in about thirty minutes. And hold on to your thought. Out of coverage area again.

He is always good for a flirt, he is a flirt. I forgot I was worried.

Notes from the 48th North

Sent: Tuesday, 24 August 2010 ~ 8.39am

The news sent me to my library of books saved from my university times. I was looking for all the definitions of the term LOVE that I ran across throughout my studies. I do remember that as students we have sunk our teeth into this concept repeatedly. But we really never felt satisfied enough that we could have agreed on one. Many definitions seemed to be true but never all inclusive.

Yet I found one definition that had stuck in my mind because it was odd, or so I thought, until I read his book: *Love is Letting Go of Fear*, by the psychiatrist Gerald G. Jampolsky (first published 1979, ISBN 0-553-23079-4). It was mostly an issue of fear for ourselves vs. turning towards the other person with concern, care, and love. Well, this all is still open to interpretation. But what I am watching right now in real life, a bit awestruck, is lending much support to the Jampolky statement.

The nation seemed to hold its breath when one of our prominent politicians announced yesterday that he will have to withdraw from his posts for a while. His wife is very ill and needs a kidney transplant. Since there are 12,000 people, so I heard, that are waiting for the same, it would take too long.

Therefore, he will donate one of his kidneys to his wife. This is the man that ran for Chancellor in 2009. He was foreign minister then, a successful career politician. He dropped it all for his wife.

What else did he say?

Jampolsky: Love is the way I walk in gratitude.

And in the Epilogue:

Let us recognize that we are united as one Self and illuminate the world with the light of Love that shines through us. Let us awaken to the knowledge that the essence of our being is Love, and, as such we are the light of the world.

Notes from the 48th North

Sent: Friday, 17 September 2010 ~ 1.16pm

A few hours earlier I watched the sun set over the hills in the west. It was a vividly red and black colored sky. The red was as screamingly intense as the black of the rainclouds. I went out into the meadow to surround myself with the vibrations of the colors, the horizon, the skyline of forests and church towers in a light late summer breeze. A term jumped into my mind: *melancholy*. When have I last felt that?! I remember only one such feeling – in Finale Ligure, Italian Riviera, at the beach in September, a long time ago. But now, why today? As I allowed nature to take me away like this I thought about my people, my loved ones and my friends that are facing difficult times or decisions, none of them here, but all of them, except one, at greater or lesser distances away. I should be there with them. I should be there out in the world where I have spent the greater part of my life. The irony occurred to me promptly: I am out in the world. I am right in the middle of it, just not at the same places that they are. You and I, we both have the chronic helper syndrome, Frau Martin. That was said by my doctor who became a colleague of sorts. We always try to be where things have gone wrong. So what is wrong with that? We both, dear doctor, could not live any other way. So let me have my melancholic moment, let my soul swing free for a while. It is not depressing, it is regenerating. After that, I will be out there again applying my chronic helper syndrome. I will get rewarded with happy moments. ... *denn die Freude, die wir geben, kehrt ins eigene Herz zurueck* (the pleasures we can give come back into our own hearts).

Spotlight on a Stream of Consciousness

Notes from the 48th North

Sent: Thursday, 23 September 2010 ~ 8.32am

Today is that special day when they both meet, halfway. They do this twice a year. It is the meeting of perfect equilibrium, perfect harmony and perfect peace. No fights, no angry exchanges. Only for one day and one night can they stay together. They know they have to move on following a law that has been established – no one knows for sure when. If they did not – well, it would not be fair. By moving on into opposite directions hardships and pleasures of life are distributed evenly. It is a give and take as it should be. I will get snow and you will get warmth and sunshine. I will be watching. As a bonus, it will be full moonlight tonight, too. Fitting for so special a happening – the 23rd of September. No melancholy tonight.

Did you know, love, that in the German language "day" is masculine – der Tag – and "night" is feminine – die Nacht? So, tonight is a perfect lover's night? Until March then, hopefully. Meanwhile, take good care of equilibrium, harmony and peace. Think of it that there is this Zauberwort in biology, and not alone there: Homeostasis.

Notes from the 48th North

Sent: Wednesday, 29 September 2010 ~ 6.13pm

For the better part of a week I have been limping through the days. My knee hurts still the same and I finally give up hope that "it will go away" by itself. Since my GP of many years has retired I have seen his successor. Liked him almost instantly and that seemed mutual and extended to my other family members (as far as they are here). He has moved to a new location together with two other docs that I have used occasionally. Brand new building, brand new praxis facilities with therapeutic, mood enhancing lighting in the waiting room. I am still standing at the reception when he comes by to pick up his next patient. You are looking good, he says with a big smile. Well thank you, doc. That is encouraging. I assume you mean this medically? He laughs loud and walks off into the treatment room. I get the same comfortable feeling – we have a wire to each other.

Fix my knee please, fast, I think I am going to travel next week. Where are you going? One hour flying, doc, so I need my meds for that as well, please. I have only one more patch. The last ones I gave you a year ago and you are already out of them? Well, when you worked all those years in Scandinavia, you had to escape winter depression, you told me. I have to escape this dreary November weather in September and perhaps I follow my calling to travel. Have been standing still since April now or at least July. He laughs. Have you read my book yet? I am ordering it. And that is our wire that connects us. Two expats trying to get a grip on "back home", trying to acclimatize to a new self-understanding. We are back and we are perhaps both not sure about this. To not be a foreigner is still strange. So I will be out of here next week to see how it feels in a foreign language these days.

Notes from the 48th North

Sent: Monday, 11 October 2010 ~ 8.21am

Eighteen years ago I left Paris to move back to Germany and on to Egypt. A week ago I returned to this City of Lights with a light heart and expectations of four fun days. I was rewarded with more than I had hoped for. This time I followed my own plan, desires and intuitions as I did not have a six year old to watch and to please. The first evening and the first following day I let myself meander and drift through the streets and alleys of downtown Paris. On the plane from Munich – a seventy-five-minute trip – I tried to dig up my rusty French. The next day I deliberately avoided English in favor of French. The next two days were filled with delight as I went through two of the great art museums of Paris (no, it was not the Louvre this time). Again, I did not have those guide books in English or German. None, I had to make it in French! But then I forgot all about language when I sat and looked at my van Goghs, eight of them in a row! I remembered the study I once did about his art and how it compared to his life in art therapy terms. These are the canvases that his hands and brushes have touched! His unhappy life came to my mind. I imagined how he might have felt when he put brush strokes on canvas. I sat there for a long time, not wanting to leave, as if I was trying to burn those originals into my memory. And then the Picassos, who needs language, who needs to be verbal when so many have so wonderfully and overwhelmingly used visual communication?

An evening dinner on the top floor restaurant of Pompidou Centre made for enjoyable conversation and a great view over the night sky of the city. The conversation went through three languages. I became aware of an uncomfortable feeling but it went as it came. However, the next day, the last day, the feeling returned. What was that? And I knew suddenly what was going on. I did not act like a tourist which is what I was. I walked around as if I had to move and start to live here again! Wasn't that always the case when I came to a new city? Interesting – will that feeling ever leave me?

Notes from the 48th North

Sent: Sunday, 24 October 2010 ~ 9.03am

There is something to be said for these dreary, overcast, foggy, drizzly, dopamine-eating November days in October. For once they get me to visit Paris, they get me an invitation to the eastern Mediterranean, to Switzerland, and to a nice hour in a Cafe in Munich.

Well, yesterday it was Erik's Gasthaus. Today, it is a pub, yes, because Anton, our Scot, is celebrating his birthday. Friends and neighbors are to come after church for a traditional Weisswurstessen – no, it is not Huggies, but the Bavarian equivalent to it. Don't tell me you want tea, Marie says with a face expressing disgust. No kid, I take a wheat beer with a slice of lemon. All right, that's better. Is Anton drinking tea? No, not him, he is a Scot. Our Cello musician starts Happy Birthday; it sounds terrible, but comes from the heart. Anton gets up and tells us the start of his Bavarian life. How he married in 1975 in this village church, with his friends from Scotland, all in kilts. How he had been tricked by his future brother-in-law introducing him to Bavarian Schnapps. It was as clear as water, Anton tells, (it always has been, it still is) an innocent-looking liquid while being very potent. Drink after drink he was given, only Luka, the terrible, did not drink Schnapps but water. It looked just the same. Anton was unsuspecting. That was the last time he had to be taken home by his wife and his brother-in-law.

Half of the forty people in the room get up and start a little play that they have secretly composed. Anton sits on the Hotchair, in the middle of the room, beaming all over his face. He has reason, too. He is liked, he is integrated. He speaks flawless and accentless German. The play is all in Bavarian, no problem for Anton. I don't know how much he also feels at home, besides his successful integration. We all have a good time. The room is full of talk and laughter, the decibels high. We are amongst ourselves, in the heartland of Bavaria, who cares about the drizzle outside. I feel really good. Nobody points me out as special anymore. I am just there like everybody else, a long lost feeling for me in this part of the world. Why does it also slightly scare me? Nobody knows (except Anton) that I have selected three Scottish poems yesterday to read to him today. I was very involved and was looking forward to teasing him a little with these Scottish writings. I had all but forgotten that only six people could understand them – Anton, his wife, and his four daughters. So I kept my poems in my purse and before I left I slipped them into my present for him. Great, he said, I will teach you the singsong when we are together some other time, just the four of us. I suspect that his core, a part of his soul, is in the Scottish Highlands. Just like my senses are still out in the world. It all is peacefully settled though, together in one soul, I think.

Notes from the 48th North

Sent: Friday, 5 November 2010 ~ 9.05pm

It was to be another mood lifting autumn day. The azure color of the sky was spotted with storm clouds. The wind was strong and gusty but southerly, and thus drove the unseasonably warm air across the Alps to warm up Munich one more time before the winter freeze. I was downtown early. I love that hour of the day when a big city wakes up. The pedestrian zone had only a few early birds in it. I was astounded to see how many dogs lived in apartments in the city center. Waiters were busy setting up tables and chairs outdoors. By noon those were all occupied with people in coats and jackets eating their lunches and drinking their coffees before everything got cold or the wind dusted it and dropped a leaf or two into the melon soup.

Still, I was glad when I stepped into the new praxis rooms of my doctor and could get out of the stormy situation. She again had found a place, not far from the old one, that occupied the top floor of the building, allowing a view over the rooftops of Munich. It was not as nice a view towards the university as the one before. I had always loved to sit in her waiting room and have all the towers of Munich, the dome, the city hall, St. Peters, the old city hall in front of me, almost bird's view. For some reason that is not quite clear to me, I have always had a fondness for the rooftop view of cities. Come to think of it, what have they been so far – Paris, Washington DC, San Francisco, Sydney, Hong Kong, Rome – but only Munich and Paris elicit that soft nostalgia that I seem to feel overlooking the roofs of those two cities. In Munich, of course, I have spent my teenage and early twenties. What fun we all had together, the risky things we did, the carefree and hopeful anticipations we all shared. It was so very great, sprinkled with a careless attitude as only early youth can have. Well, that must be the reason, the associations that it has with friends who could not afford anything else but a bohemian flat. That, to be sure, was not always fun per se. Paris rooftops remind me of poverty stricken painters, hope, and love life – how can that be nice? It is connected to one of those stories by that Hungarian author whose name starts with Gabor (shame on me). It is "Monpti", made into a movie with Romy Schneider and Horst Buchholz, both classics now, the book and the movie. The twists and turns my mind makes amaze even me.

But the city of Munich, I noticed that it is growing on me again. I felt more at home, more belonging yesterday, not so much the I-am-visiting-I-am-back feeling. No, it was more like I know this place, I am from here. Weird! Don't know what to do with it, how to integrate it. No problem, I will allow the feeling to take its course in a wait and see fashion. To top it off though, between dome and city hall I met a woman from BIS whom I last saw ten years ago. She was so surprised I remembered her name. The inevitable question: Are you visiting or are you here to stay? My answer was the truth: Don't know for sure.

Actually, people seem to have problems associating me with geographical stability. Even my doctor (I see her for check ups regularly, and have done so for the last twenty-three years) asked me yesterday in confusion: Where are you now, oh that's right, you are here now! Have you been anywhere this year? Where? Dubai and Maldives in one swoop, Beirut, Berlin, Paris and counting. Good grief, she says, I have been in London. Good for you, doctor, that is almost as good as being here in Munich.

Notes from the 48th North

Sent: Saturday, 13 November 2010 ~ 8.16am

We were in the departure lounge, boarding pass ready, waiting for the call to board the plane. CM jiggled one of his legs to the music in his ears. He was ready for the tropical islands, so was I. No, not Hawaii, don't know where actually. Somewhere in the Indian Ocean perhaps. But Papa was not here yet. My tension was increasing. He should be here by now. Any moment we were going to be called up for boarding. There it was! CM heard it somehow. He stood up and moved forward to join the line of passengers. I turned back, desperately looking for him. CM had moved forward but was still this side of the gate. We cannot leave, I thought, we cannot leave without him. I turned around to call CM back. We were not taking off, we were not complete. But CM was not in line anymore. He was already on the runway, taking off. I am terrified. This kid cannot go off alone into the Tropics! He does not even have any money with him, does not know the name of the hotel. What is he going to do? I must go back to Dubai to find my husband, or, no, I must follow CM. There, damn it, what took you so long? It is too late. He is gone. We just take the next plane, he said calmly. CM is grown up, he will be okay. Even in my dreams I am traveling! Yesterday I had a nice Facebook exchange with Kaku, the hermit crab from the Maldives. Come on over, she invited me, when the weather is bugging you. Perhaps that was the stimulus for that awful dream.

Notes from the 48th North

Sent: Monday, 15 November 2010 ~ 8.59am

She was the organist of our church for almost four decades. She was my mentor in choir singing. We have always had a special relationship for some reason. I helped her decorate the altar for Easter or other religious festivities. For that she would slip a few coins into my pocket, into the pocket of a schoolgirl and advised conspiratorially: Don't tell my nieces. I felt special and proud. And then I went into my teenage years, my voice changed. But she let me stay on until it was time for me to leave the village for a boarding school in Munich. That was the end of that. Later, as an adult, when I came back from the US to visit she was always happy to see me. She had not changed her protective interest in me. Our relationship was still special. I don't think I have ever left without her calling after me: Come again, Isolde. Now I have lived here again for more than a year and thus I run into her occasionally. Come visit me, Isolde, is her refrain now. Yes, I will, is my promise. But the *I did not have time* phrase when I saw her the next time, like a few weeks ago in the pub for Anton's birthday, felt shallow and uncaring. You did not come, I was waiting for you, she greeted me later with controlled accusation. She is lonesome, I thought, despite her five children she has borne and raised. She is 88-years old, good looking, if you know what I mean, and very sharp in her mind. Last Sunday, after my power-walk, I swung by her house. I have been waiting for you, she greeted me. We had a great visit reminiscing about our choir days together when I was a little girl, and when she was a little girl and a young teenager during WWII, and when she got hit the first time in first grade by her theology teacher (those things hurt much more than just physically and the brain stores the insult a lifetime), about our religious upbringing and what became of it, or better, what we thought about it now, and the 180 degree turn of her view about out of wedlock pregnancies. She was so honest about her conclusions in matters of religion and accepted mine without a blink of an eye. She can remember the times that I was trying to research about this village and my mother's folks for my next book. She is an enormous wealth of knowledge and has no problem recalling it! Bring the old pictures next time, she offered. I tell you who the people in it are. Should I also come to play your Muehle game? She laughs and says that she would like that since her children and her next door neighbors have trouble winning against her. They hesitate to play with me, she laughs. I know I won't win either, but I can give you a hard time, I reassured her. She responded with a knowing smile. When you come ring the door bell three times, she says. I intend to, I will have time. Grand old lady, your name, Regina, suits you well.

Notes from the 48th North

Sent: Sunday, 21 November 2010 ~ 1.59am

It is Sunday morning – a typical late November morning with overcast skies, dreary, foggy, too dark for the hour of the day. It is so quiet that I can hear my nerves fire. I will have a leisurely breakfast, make it the main meal today. I light the tall, red candle on the table. Yes, I do, even when I am by myself. I just learned from L'Oreal commercials that I am worth it. All together it feels romantic and good, albeit I am aware of the solitude. But this will only be until Wednesday. At least that was what I was told. Music, ever so faintly, reaches my ear. What is that? It's getting louder, rapidly. It's a Bavarian march, a subdued one though. And I remember – today is Memorial Day, like each third Sunday in November. The parade of men is heading up the steps to the Monument of the Unknown Soldier. Two of the dignitaries carry wreaths. The veterans, the firemen and a few other delegations bring their huge, heavy, richly embroidered flags. No, I don't go to that ceremony anymore. I have been at every one of them all my childhood long.

I cannot bear the memories of my mother, one of my veteran uncles, and others around me crying when the song I once had a comrade. He marched on my side in the same step, until he fell … is being played. Three shots salute made the people jump. I think that's when I started to become a pacifist. I feel some guilt chickening out like that, but I will go up there later, when everybody is gone including my touch of anger at the idiocy of it all, and have my quiet vigil. Once again I'll read the plates with all the names on it, one being another uncle of mine that I have never met. But for now I go and watch Ludwig, the cannoniere, for the three shots salute. He walks a few steps away from the canon, dragging a cable, the trigger button in his hand. He tilts his head away, pulls his shoulders up and hunches over, presses the button. A tremendous bang makes the heart vibrate, a long flame shoots out of the barrel. The echo comes back from the nearby forest, a lot of blue smoke drifts away. Two more times ...

I am not the first pacifist of my nation. There is one that I hold in high esteem. He was our emperor Friedrich II, during the Crusades in the eleventh century. He went to the Holy Land in an attempt to persuade his Muslim counterpart to allow access for Christians to biblical land and Jerusalem. He succeeded – by human contact, persuasion skills perhaps, and without the strike of a sword. He spoke, so historians wrote, six languages, amongst them perfect Arabic. Perhaps he just had an accepting attitude. Why else would he have brought back "sciences" from there as well? That might even figure from another point, too. He was a Third Culture Kid, born in Palermo, Sicily, a kingdom that reached way up the Italian boot in those days. His mother was a Sicilian, his father from the northern German dynasty of the Staufers. Eventually this man went back home to Palermo and died there of an infectious disease.

This afternoon my cousin is coming to pick me up to go to another village to enjoy the first "Advent Market" of the season, a Christmas fair. I want to see the local arts and crafts. He is driving so that I can have my Gluehwein, hot and spicy. Surely there will be somebody with another cup of that beverage in his hands talking about "the war back then" when he was a grade-schooler. Trauma has to be revisited at least on that particular day of the year.

Notes from the 48th North

Sent: Sunday, 28 November 2010 ~ 3.58pm

The weather and road conditions were such that I considered moving this dinner to the next weekend. Don't want to endanger friends. They would have to drive for almost two hours over winterish highways. No, they said, we will come, tomorrow it will be a blue sky day and the roads will have been cleared. Well, you know the treacherous and tricky patches through forest and over bridges, etc. To slow down from, well you know ... high speed, just be careful then, no matter when you arrive. Dinner can wait. We will have the rest of the day.

They came! We have lived as neighbors and friends in one place close to Munich. Each of us left there twelve years ago. Meanwhile we have reunited maybe three times. The connection lasted. Now two of our kids live in close proximity to each other in Berlin. And so it went. We had our Thanksgiving Dinner together, talked and laughed, exchanging stories written by our lives, rehashed old times, exchanged notes about our kids that have left home, talked about our aches and pains, felt better because we go the same course of life, enjoyed each other's company immensely. It was as if we had never separated, twelve years ago. It was about wonderful people, a wonderful friendship that lasted over time and geographical distance. It was dark when they left, to drive back on winter road conditions. Have to be at a handball game tomorrow, they said. Have a safe trip, send note when you are home. When should we meet again? Perhaps in Berlin, together with our kids, they suggest. I am all for it!

Notes from the 48th North

Sent: Wednesday, 1 December 2010 ~ 2.56am

Do you want to spend a few days with me in London – you know, art gallery, backstage London and all? You bet I do! When? Wednesday morning. Let's book it, flight, backstage and all. But are you sure you can hold up? Mind your cold, your Monday trip to Berlin, your cold and your Tuesday trip to Geneva, and then Wednesday off to GB? Ah, yeah, no problem. Okay, let's do it then.

Taxi arrives 5.30am Monday to take him to the airport. Give my son a hug. 8.00am my telephone rings: I can't go, missed my flight, drive was sloshy and treacherous, terrible, the next flights are cancelled – weather too bad for landing in Berlin.

10.00am he is back. Well, let's treat your cold instead!

Tuesday you can take my car to MUC as you are going to be back in the evening. The Tuesday sky is azzurro blue, have a good flight and a successful meeting in Geneva. 10.00am telephone rings. I am coming home. The flight has been cancelled as Geneva is wrapped up in snowstorms, planes can't land. Well, good, should I prepare some chicken soup and sage tea to treat your bronchitis? Yeah, please! Even with tea? Yes, please ("what the Bavarians drink to cure their colds is harmful to a non-Bavarian"). He must really feel bad!

Tomorrow they predict the Geneva storm and snow moving northward to Munich and on up. Do we really have to go to London? We will either not be able to leave Munich or get stuck on Friday in Heathrow. No, no, it will be all right. Well, I will check with the airline before we leave here. Actually, come to think of it, I would rather not go. Do you mind if I cancel my flight? No, go ahead, but

I have to go. Need to leave the house at 7.00am Okay, you can have my car. If you are not back by tomorrow evening I will buy myself a new one. Wednesday morning this otherwise sanguine personality sits a bit gloomy looking at the breakfast table.

Fuck, he says.

Notes from the 48th North

Sent: Thursday, 9 December 2010 ~ 3.34am

I must be really sick – I am drinking tea for four days now. So he spoke incredulously. Yep, I agree, for you, my dear, that would be an indicator of your wellbeing or the absence of it. Not only that, you even don't ask about the kind of tea anymore. You have accepted sage tea, fennel tea, black tea, green tea with apple and Ginko, bronchitis tea, lime tree tea – did I miss one? You also omitted your usual comment of YUCK! just at the offer of tea. When we were at the doctor's you looked from him to me, suspiciously though, which triggered the good man to point his finger at me saying: We have not talked on the phone beforehand, it is not a conspiracy. You stay put for two weeks, out of airplanes, or face three weeks of hospital! Here are the drops to help your cough and here is the antibiotic – no choice here. – Now you are getting better, have accepted a glass of beer and booked your flight. As one coffee and one tea drinker we have made it together for a long time. That is not any issue. But the real question that arose from this predicament is no longer a question: We need a winter retreat further south, at least until it is time for skiing.

Notes from the 48th North

Sent: Tuesday, 14 December 2010 ~ 7.12pm

Three weeks ago the heavens opened up to send us showers of snow. The slow silent down drift looked so nice, the white covered landscape seemed a symphony of peace and silence. Then the stormy, wind driven snow drifts came in spectacular waves. This all with short intervals of sun that gave the snow that diamond sprinkled look. The social consequence of early winter weather was marked by solidarity and fun, only short of building a village snowman. At 6.00am I can hear my robust neighbors scratching and shoveling outside. Later I join them. Isolde, is that you? Albert yells across the fence. Better late than never, he comments. Are you kidding me, Albert, I don't own a store. Do you need any help? Of course, come on over and bring your shovel. I can hear the tractor from my neighbor to the north. Rea, when you are finished with your lot, could you please clear my driveway? No problem, Isolde. She comes right away, drives her tractor with the rusty snowplough three or four times the length of our driveway and is done. Thank you, you saved me from frozen fingers! That's just it. Gradually the deep freeze and the other downsides of winter are gaining the upper hand over the romantic feelings. How long is this going to last? Is it the sixth time today that I am doing my daily exercise at -10, not to speak of night temps below that which kept me from standing out on the balcony at night to watch a meteorite shower. My eyes are watering outside from the freezing cold, the car runs funny for a while before it warms up. This is for the birds, I am getting fed up. And I am having second thoughts about living so far north of the equator. Pictures of going swimming every morning with my friends in the desert regions of the world flash up. Sharm el-Sheikh appears in front of my mental eye, or Italy, south of Rome. Winters in LA were a piece of cake and if one felt like snow and skiing it took only a short flight and a drive up the Sierras. So, California perhaps, again? Where would I be happier? Feel a little like a traitor thinking that, though. It is also true that I missed these winters when I was residing southward, admittedly for a week or two, not months. Can't decide yet. I am in limbo.

Notes from the 48th North

Sent: Saturday, 18 December 2010 ~ 5.16pm

It is a beautiful, full moon, starry sky winter night. I was just out on my balcony to look into the nightly heavens. Orion, the most prominent companion of sleep-interrupted desert nights of Arabia, was up there in its full magnificence. And it is bitterly cold out there, -14C the weather woman on TV said. It was not quite as chilly yesterday morning, but plenty still to keep the snow powdery. Thank you, that made my work, clearing the driveway and footpaths much easier. Each morning there are tracks in front of the door and going on to the barn, of a four-toes animal with claws. It is an Illtis (is it a polecat in English?), the guy with the mink like fur, also the guy that will bite through cables underneath cars.

But this is not the only nocturnal action out there. There is at least one cat and one large dog judging by the size of the paw prints in the snow. They all follow the paths that I have shovelled free. Glad to be of service, you are welcome on the premises. Just leave the hedgehog that sleeps behind the garage under a board leaning against the wall and under the leaves from the walnut tree alone. I thought he was in hibernation. Yet there are tracks going into his den. Perhaps somebody else lives there. KK told me yesterday at length about the three different species of birds that came in a flash to share, or fight over, a slice of bread. That reminded me that I had not put out the bird feeding house, nor did I hang any feeder rings. With a of snow, or even less, the non-migrating birds can use a little assistance.

Herb's young dog loves the snow and does not mind the cold. He looks like a German Shepherd, but Herb told me that his genes have been mixed with a Golden Retriever's. The latter is only visible at a closer look. Regardless, he is a mostly black beauty in the white snow. He stands in the deep snow, in front of his master, waiting for every shovel of snow that Herb throws, obviously intentionally, high into the air. The dog jumps into it and snaps a mouthful of snow midair.

A sentence out of a book, perhaps it was *Trinity* by Leon Uris, about the recent history of Ireland, comes to my mind: For Ireland is a terrible beauty. Something like that I could attribute to this winter as well. Or the ying and the yang, the good and the bad, the two sides of one coin, and so forth. Yesterday the good side of winter was up, definitely. I love to hear the noise the children make when they are out there with their sleds, speeding down slopes, rolling bodily in the snow. And look at the snowmen appearing side by side with the outdoor Christmas trees. I admit having thought about building a snowman myself. Asking my cousin to help me, he laughed and asked me whether I am not finished with my childhood. Go on, be this way then, stiff and tight like an adult.

I am getting carried away!

Notes from the 48th North

Sent: Friday, 31 December 2010 ~ 1.04pm

Bringing Anton, the treasurer, a box of Lebanese sweets for their Christbaum Auction turned into a two hour delightful English tea time. This can easily happen when you go to see Anton and his wife. So, are you coming to the Auction then? He asked us both. Yes, this year we will come. After all, I have not exercised such a Bavarian tradition for aeons. That auction is as Bavarian as it can get. It is called "Christmas tree auction". Anton's neighbor is the auctioneer. He is pretty good at it, too, fast, tricky and humorous. And it all started out with our children's choir singing Jingle Bells, mixed lyrics, English and German. Then there was a second Bavarian Christmas song of old, old times. Steven tried, but gave up. Takes a native to sing that. I am surrounded by my schoolmates and one of my mates from the choir when I was a kid here. I thought I can feel a connection and the memory come across the table from her.

Interesting! Andreas is auctioning off one bottle of wine, one glass of local honey, one box of Ferrero Kuesschen, one wood carved figure and more. And that, he announces, are Turkish sweets – three Euros, who offers more? Silence. They are really good, original, great gift, great taste. Hesitantly the offers come in. We take it, the four of us! one young man finally shouts. They open it immediately, examine the contents. At the end of the evening they had but a few cookies left. Isolde are they from you and Steve? Yeah, how did you guess? But now comes the donation part, "buying" the Christmas tree and donating it right back so that someone else can "buy it" again. Andreas shouts the name of each buyer by way of thanking him or her. A wicked thought occurs to me. This man has come by way of marriage into the village long after I had left. We have met off and on during those summer festivals, or during New Year's Eve historical pistol shooting, but not more than loosely. He does not really know me. I offer a donation holding up my money. He turns to me and shouts my name from the time I was a kid, the name of our house and my first name. He did not blink an eyelash. I shout in surprise, did not expect it at all. Of course, I know "all that" he grins into my face. I think he knew what I had been up to. Everybody laughed out loud at my noisy reaction of astonishment. But that laughter! I heard kindness, friendship, acceptance, neighborliness, familiarity, perhaps inclusion back into their circle that they have never left? Perhaps we have found the way back to each other. Perhaps we can accept the different plateau on which we can meet now.

Notes from the 48th North

Sent: Friday, 7 January 2011 ~ 5.19pm

Yesterday morning the rain falling on frozen ground created sheets of sparkling ice on roads, pedestrian walks and everywhere. This was also the situation fifteen years ago, when I went out and broke my hip. But today is today, no PTSD after so long. But the similarity of the situation increased my heartbeat and caused me stepping up caution. It did not let me ignore the memory. Should I keep this dental appointment today or not? The salt truck has come by twice already. It should be safe enough. I decided not to give in to things from the past. I drove like on raw eggs and, likewise, in the city walked like on raw eggs, placing my steps carefully only on gravel. Did you make it okay? The dentist asked. Yeah, but do you actually want me here? I have a scratchy throat? He put on his mask and his gloves. Sure, he said, you are not the only one. We will clean, polish, and seal, then you will be done for another six months. That's a word, doc, it was worth the anxiety about the treacherous, dangerous road conditions. Besides, I feel heroic, having made it and having overpowered my ego that tried to keep me back.

But at home the cold came out more. The usual symptoms, throat ache, head ache, bone ache (a little). I felt so good, this is not fair! At night sleep was pitiful. I had been awake already for hours with a fitful drifting off in between. Listening into the nightly silence I realized again that the sounds of my childhood were absent. As a child I had my cold and my flu every winter. I used to be awake at night just the same. Mother would bring me a cup of tea and rub some Eucalyptus cream on my chest. I could hear a dog barking from a farm half an hour walking time away. Another one would answer. I knew which dogs they were and loved the sound. At four in the morning, when I was either still awake or woke up again, it was still a dark. But the roosters, our own and our neighbors, were crowing already. Those sounds have vanished. Nowadays dogs are supposed to not bark disturbingly until people get up. Hardly anybody keeps chickens anymore. The barking and the crowing were comforting to me. It meant safe stability. The world was okay, familiar and predictable. Curious how I then came to live a most unstable life!

I think I need some TLC (tender loving care) today.

Notes from the 48th North

Sent: Wednesday, 12 January 2011 ~ 8.46am

His voice was so full of feelings of fun and pleasure. At 9.00am he called me to share his experience with me, making me envious as well. After all, I have been at the foot of this mountain, crossing the pass to Baalbeck in Lebanon. But that was in the summer. Now it was winter there. We must come here to ski, just once, he said then. Well, he made it, today was the day! And he loved it, I could hear it. Some men collect so-called trophy women, I was told over and over again. But some collect trophy ski runs! He counted it out every winter: Germany, Austria, Switzerland, Italy, Turkey, California, Colorado, New Zealand, and now Lebanon. Confronted with that, he said, But I have a trophy woman. And I have a skier, topping Jean Claude Killy and Carl Schranz put together.

Best flirt of the snow seasons – my husband, like Jean Claude Killy and Carl Schranz together.

Notes from the 48th North

Sent: Wednesday, 12 January 2011 ~ 10.48am

This has been turning around in my left frontal lobe (or my amygdalla) since it happened. But did not really know what I wanted to express. Now I am clearer. I am a proud mom. You see, my son has been bugging me for about a year to see Avatar. When I questioned the wisdom, need, or necessity of this I was told about the fantastic technology used for the first time in that movie and that it was such great a film. Thus it would not be good for my image and self respect if I had not seen it. Finally, at one evening during the past holidays son prepared everything for mother to watch *Avatar* right after dessert. I gave in. But by now I was curious about this film for another reason: Why was it so important to him that mom sees this movie? Daddy had seen it with him long before. Was that not enough? Perhaps watching that blasted film will give me a hint. And didn't I know that nice experiences should be shared with people we love and appreciate! It was so great! And the greatest of it all was that my son wanted me to see this. Can't leave mom behind the times, can you? Who cares about the reasons anyway? My son wanted me to see Avatar and ENYOY IT! And I did for reasons overt and covert. Thanks a million my son and do it again!

Notes from the 48th North

Sent: Saturday, 29 January 2011 ~ 5.11am

Last night, after my 3.00am computer session, I fell asleep again to get my beneficial and necessary REM sleep and an accompanying, terrible dream. When I realized that I was awake now, I felt great relief – *it is not true!* I still had my purse, my driver's license, my credit cards, my car, and my identity. I was not lost. In my dream all of these items had been stolen from me, leaving me stranded, alone in a foreign place, probably Dubai. I did not even have the phone numbers to block my credit cards from abuse. I panicked and still felt that for a few seconds after I woke up.

I have never been a follower of Freudian style dream interpretation. But I do believe that the conclusions a person draws from a dream are good therapeutic material. So what was I to make of this nightmarish dream? Why the fear, the feeling of threat? Then I remembered that the panic came up when I realized I had nothing to prove my identity, nobody knew me in this foreign land. It was like I did not exist, like I was a nobody. Awake, I opened my pocket book to see that all my items that could prove my identity were there. I did not consult my passport, though. That one already felt uncomfortable when I picked it up a few months ago. It is a brand new one with no stamp or visa in it whatsoever. I have used it only once since it was issued when I went to Paris. Don't get a stamp anymore at that border because it is EU. My old passport and several before were full of visas and entry stamps. I do not like a blank passport. It is like part of my history has been ignored. Traveling first time abroad? No, sir! But I know all of that, have been through it before, every passport had filled up again. What is my problem – my old and familiar identity issue revisiting? Unfortunately, that thought hit home!

Two days ago I pulled the monthly magazine of the municipality out of my mailbox. To my great surprise the front cover showed one of my nature pictures that I had sent to the mayor (we had met out in the field each with camera in hand) two years ago. He had once flashed it onto the screen at the beginning and end of an assembly back then. Long ago, out of mind. But now that picture had resurfaced on the front page. I had not been consulted, neither was my name printed as the photographer. I still don't know what to make of it. Is it careless disregard or a great honor? I have settled for the latter. But I am still puzzled about it. There is another connotation. I was not identified but kept anonymous. So am I accepted and integrated back into the insider circle? I am back on the local Totem pole?

Ambivalence, my old friend, is back as well. I feel comfortable about my roots. But between my felt identity, acquired over so many years and so much hardship as well as wonderful adventures as a foreigner, and my likely Totem pole position amongst my (loving, tolerant, and accepting) people are a few worlds, a few continents, many countries and many years apart. Mostly and more importantly there is also my identity that I feel so comfortable with that a dream about losing it can be called a nightmare. No doubt, I will have to come to terms with this.

Notes from the 48th North

Sent: Saturday, 5 February 2011 ~ 8.45am

It was an unbelievable six years ago that I have left Cairo. But now, under the circumstances, the four years that I have spent there stood up in front of my mental eyes again as if I had left yesterday. All the places I have frequented, like the Khan el-Khalili, the Corniche along the Nile, the Christmas concert with my colleagues at the opera house, the cafe in the old part of Cairo where Nagib Machfus read his newspaper and had his coffee on a daily basis, the Mena House, and, of course, the Pyramids; they all have vivid colors and life again in my mind. And, oh yes, the unforgettable performance of Aida one moderately cool or warm night, out in the desert, to the west of the Great Pyramids of Ghiza, is ringing in my ears afresh. The Pyramids functioned as background to the stage and the full moon stood low on the horizon as background for the Pyramids. Imagine the picture!

So do the people reappear in my mind. Via a phone call I have found my only colleague left there. She and her husband were safe. There are others, out of my day to day Egyptian life, there that I have no way of contacting. There is one I particularly would want to know about. She was my Arabic teacher. Over time we became friends of sorts. At first we used to seek each other out to talk. There was a curiosity about the other one's lifestyle, so different, so exotic. When the talks moved into more and more personal issues we found ourselves laughing in surprise. We felt alike, often exactly the same. But our outlook on life, our expectations for our future, were very different. Our dreams may have been similar, but the pursuit of them and the issue of realizing them – well, sometimes a small world separated us. And yet, without realizing it, a special bond of friendship had developed between us. I guess it was instigated by our mutual total trust and the open, daring comparisons of our personal lives. No, I have never seen her hair because I only met her in the presence of others around. But when my last week in Cairo came around, she asked to go to a restaurant together. I agreed instantly. We needed a special goodbye, just the two of us. I think we knew it was most likely the avenue of no return. I have not heard or seen her since. So she is the one I am concerned about, probably unnecessarily so. She is embedded in her family and protected, I am sure. When everything has returned to calm I will make some phone calls. Perhaps I am lucky. I miss the contact with her.

Notes from the 48th North

Sent: Tuesday, 15 February 2011 ~ 5.33pm

I will join you later, after I am finished here, I tell them. They are off to the forest to cut trees, those that are sick with bugs under their rind (bark), those that are good for firewood. I hurry with my task. Have been in the house and on the computer half the day already, need to get out for some fresh air and my exercise routine. The morning was wrapped into thick fog. Now, at 1.00pm it has thinned out. As I walk down the dirt road everything looks like a gentle, gray veil has descended on hills and valleys, giving the forest a mysterious Hansel and Gretel appearance. Yesterday seven deer – actually they were seven does – appeared out of the haze and jumped across the road, in front of my car. So I scan for that as I walk. There is no wind at all. It is eerily silent around me. Until I enter the forest and hear the chain saw. I am heading in the direction from which that ugly sound comes from. That's where they are. Suddenly it stops. It is silent again. Since all the snow had melted a week ago, the forest is saturated with different shades of green. The floor is covered with moss. It even crawls up the tree trunks. My steps meet soft, almost springy ground. And the air – the forest air – it is mind liberating to me! The soil of a pine tree forest smells very pleasant and the moss has its own distinct scent. I have liked this since childhood times and it still has the same notion of "free" to me.

Have you ever watched a twenty-five-metre tall pine tree fall after it has been cut? For some reason it touches me emotionally to the point of tears. It is a breathtaking sight for me, every time. It starts to tilt earthward very slowly, like an avalanche. Then it picks up speed, a hushing, rustling sound comes up, twigs fall to the ground, pine cones may drop. With thunder the giant tree hits the floor. Its top swings a few more times up and down, and then everything is still. Thirty, forty or fifty years of growth have been eliminated by a person, so very much smaller and weaker than the tree, and a chain saw, within the space of five minutes.

Now I am standing by the fox hole. It has three additional exits. I wonder whether the fox is inside while we work more or less noisily around his den. Carefully KK drives his tractor around the biggest hole. I like him for it. He has to pull the trees out into the clearing. We cut them into one-metre logs. I help to load them onto the trailer, at least the thinner, lighter ones. This is weight bearing exercise, the therapy to prevent my osteoporosis. No fitness studio could ever match this one in the forest! It is time to go home. Job done, I held up well. Steven and I walk slowly but happily along the southern edge of the forest. Here comes Gerda with Ramses, her Great Dane. She puts him on a leash when she sees us coming. The other dog, a mixture of English sheep dog, Berner Sennenhund, and what could be a German Shepherd, is the new addition. This one always runs fiercely, barking alongside the fence, when I walk by. Just walk by, she says reassuringly to us. I have them firmly in my hands. Steven has switched sides and walks on the dog side. This gesture is a Valentine's Day present, all right. I would not trade it for anything.

Is it today? I am being asked. Yes!

Spotlight on a Stream of Consciousness

Notes from the 48th North

Sent: Saturday, 19 Feb 2011 ~ 8.57pm

He called me from Paris telling me that he is on the way to the airport. I'll be home about halfway to midnight. So he hoped. The same driver who has taken him to and from the airport and through the nerve testing traffic of the City of Lights so many times is safely delivering him back to Charles de Gaulle this time as well. Very comfortable, when you can sink exhausted from meetings into the seat of that car with so trusted and familiar a driver. Even though these two men had a hard time finding a common language to communicate in, over time a relationship developed. Au revoir, goodbye, auf Wiedersehen, till next time – may I? The driver hands him a box of French sweets! How nice, but why? Merci! *But how to tell this man that I cannot take this into the cabin of a plane?* He only had a briefcase; it was only a one day trip. Can't check in the sweets without a suitcase. He called Colleen. She talked to the driver. Colleen will take the sweets to Lebanon on her next visit to Beirut and bring them to hand them over to the rightful recipient. In that case, nice, helpful woman, could you also take the bottle of wine that our business partner handed to me after the meeting? I cannot take that into the cabin either. Sure, no problem, she said. So both presents, in a few weeks will fly to Beirut, handed over, and he will fly them back to Germany. Can't wait to get my hands on such well traveled presents that arrived after an odyssey to find the owner.

Notes from the 48th North

Sent: Wednesday, 23 February 2011 ~ 6.31pm

I have written about this before and I am doing it again. It is just so thrilling and never gets old to me. I have been sky watching again – out on the balcony – at night, naturally, at -15 C, not naturally. I did not watch as long as I wanted to as the binoculars seemed to freeze onto my fingers. The air was biting cold but crystal clear and completely still. The stars were so incredibly bright as they usually are at such a special winter's night. Thanks to the petitions we have filed, on paper and verbally, the municipality has dimmed the street lights enough to let them come out again. Still is not the blinking carpet up there that I have seen during my childhood here. But it is, as always, the mind lifting, awe inspiring experience that it always was. Can't see Orion right now, my steady companion from the Arabian Desert. It is so very silent, it oozes utter peace, it makes me feel part of the universe, it makes me feel my insignificance and yet a necessary part of the world. My problems seem laughable by comparison. And I miss the people I love or have loved to share this with. Night sky watching puts my life in perspective. I love the view because it is just grand and hard to comprehend, well, just astronomical. But now, get back inside, quickly! Will be a while before I warm up and fall asleep again because he is skiing in the mountains of Lebanon. What did you see in the sky there? You must have seen the beams of my eyes falling on that star that is always so close to the moon.

Notes from the 48th North

Sent: Wednesday, 16 March 2011 ~ 12.42pm

It was such a fulfilling, satisfying, rewarding visit. My reception and welcome was warm hearted and compassionate, really genuine. Even those that once kept some distance between us hugged me tightly. At the time I only enjoyed being in the midst of my group and my friends again. It felt like I had not left. And I let the feeling be and enjoyed the situation. But now being back home I wonder about the vibrations that seemed to float in the air between us. I reflect on our talks. One question frequently asked is still ringing in my ears: How is it back home? Have you settled? This is an issue that every long-term expat once will have to face, sooner or later. In my travel diary that a very wise and understanding friend of mine gave me, the first page that I filled with my thoughts in Dubai has a sentence on top that goes deep into my soul: *Do not go where the path may lead, go instead where there is no path and leave a trail* (Ralph Waldo Emerson). Maybe that's it, I am a trail blazer! Have I settled? No! I don't want to. I can be content and happy many places. But settle – I am not sure I know how to do that anymore. And that is okay for me.

Notes from the 48th North

Sent: Thursday, 24 March 2011 ~ 10.29pm

After the somewhat stormy visit to Dubai being home seemed like having fallen into a social vacuum. What to do? Luckily, there is Eva's bi-annual concert. Of course! And SM and CM are flying in at the same time, I will buy three tickets for sure. Great! Everything is good timing and falls neatly into place. Eva is a home grown internationally recognized organist and pianist and we are so proud of her. She does a special, almost loving job for her fellow people. No need to go to the Munich Philharmonic. Her concerts are second to none. Vienna Spring is the theme for her pieces played this time. Oh, good evening, you are here, too, oh and you, concert instead of skiing? Hello Josef, nice to see you here ... and so it goes before we all finally settle down in our seats. Son is one row in front of us chatting away with his neighbor. Suddenly Eva's mom is beside us. She and her husband, my optician, sitting in the same row just a few seats to the middle: Frau Martin, good evening, and the whole family is here! she says with a big smile. How did it go in Dubai with your book? Before I can ask she tells me: I know everything! Can one buy this book? I am overcoming my surprise and see my opportunity. But it is in English, is it difficult to read? she adds doubtfully. But Eva can read it. I will bring you one to the store, I offer. Time to sit down, the lights are going out. Succumb to Hayden, Mozart, Schubert, Liszt and Beethoven. She has selected well and she has a few words to say about the history and peculiarities of each of the composers or the piece she will play. During break the audience collects in the cafe for the glass of champagne, courtesy of the pianist and the municipality. At the end Eva brings down the house again. She had played flawlessly. Of course, we expected no less, she has won prizes already as a teenager. Four curtains she accepted, after that it was ended by the lights coming on brightly.

Well guys, did you enjoy yourself. Yes, very much. So, I am to get the tickets for the fall concert as well? Yes, if we can fly in on time for it. The story of my life – only my family needs a plane to attend a concert

Notes from the 48th North

Sent: Monday, 4 April 2011 ~ 8.42am

It is a beautifully rainy day, and I am stuck with my story. This is a good day to do some research and visit Regina. I have to make good on my promise to bring pictures of long ago, those that are brownish-yellow and don't shine. Some of them have been visited by silverfish nasties.

Would you like coffee?

No, thanks, I am fine.

You brought pictures! She took the biggest one out of my hands. It is a so called school picture from 1931.

Do you know anybody in it? I ask.

Of course, she says, I know them all!

She positions herself next to me – closer to the light. This is Anna, and this is Lotte, and this is Frieda and this must be, no wait, yes, this is Ursula. And this is Rosa and this is Alois. Wait! Are you sure? Of course I am sure, she says with a questioning glance at me. I stare at them, the heroes of my story. After she has had enough indulgence in her childhood she puts the picture aside.

The telephone rings. She has it set on speaker phone. Mom, where have you been yesterday night at 10.45pm? I called and called and you never came to the phone! Well, I don't know, she answers slowly, where could I have been? But you never answered the phone, where you in church, where were you? I recognize the voice as one of her son's. I probably was asleep and did not hear it ringing, she offers as an explanation. Regina, tell him it is none of his business what his mother does at night. She laughs. Who is with you, Mom? It is Isolde, we are looking at old pictures. And I am reading post cards to her because she cannot read them. What do you mean Isolde cannot read? he asks puzzled. Silly, his mom says, it is old German writing. The postcards are from the turn of the century, from eighteen to nineteen hundred I mean. And she does read them to me, fluently. That way we discover that a relative of her family had a crush on one of my family. We laugh like two conspirators. I have to show that to the other Regine, a generation younger. It must have been her father.

So I did get my caffeine free coffee anyways. Can't frustrate a lady her age. She brings a huge piece of cake, the sort with whipped cream. This is a birthday cake, Regina. Is it your birthday? A few days ago, she said hesitantly. I am 89 now.

Well, we enjoy the Kaffeeklatsch. It is time to leave. I give her a kiss. She has taught me to read music. But now she refuses to use her piano. We could have even more fun together. She says the piano is not good anymore. I step outside and Fritz is there. Regina, do I have to put out your garbage can for tomorrow? His eyes focus on my hand with all the pictures. Were you looking at old pictures? He pulls out the school picture. Is my mother on here? Next time we will invite him too. Then we don't have to start over again.

Notes from the 48th North

Sent: Sunday, 10 April 2011 ~ 9.04am

My schoolmates from grade school – I think they are finally starting to believe that I am here to stay. Repeated invitations to come along seem to confirm that. Anton's group is staging a concert, Isolde, do you want to come? Yes, I do, it was so nice, educating and sophisticated last time. The so called "Music Summer between Inn and Salzach Rivers" has obviously started. I am having more and more fun with these small stage concerts in historical buildings in provincial cities. They are cozy and romantic, we drink something nice during the performance, get to know the neighbor in the next seat. Yesterdays concert was in an old, renovated train station. Great acoustics. And the musicians are of high standing – not every one there is a member of the Munich Philharmonic. And they talk to the audience quite casually, explaining and offering anecdotes. Was Franz Liszt the womanizer that later went into a monastery in Rome?

And those two guys, one with the violin and the other with his accordion brought Edith Piaf and Paris to us. I was floating on clouds reminiscing. Through the wide, high arched windows one could see the light of the still active train station, trains coming by, picking up one or two travelers. They probably went to a pop concert. Or was it Pierre, the clochard whoI saw? Make no mistake, at the end they showed their talents and their calling in the field of classical music: Hungarian Dances. And you remember Isolde? Anton's wife said to a couple. Hi, how are you Isolde? Who are they? I know them for sure? Where did I meet them? I searched my brain frantically and it did not let me down. That's right, the Scots, the dinner last summer. Hello, nice to see you again. During intermission the gentleman steps a little closer, lowering his voice as if we were conspirators: Have you settled here for good now?

I struggled for a truthful answer. I think so, yes, that is probably correct.

It is over, it was bravo, bravissimo! Maria and I talk our way out the door. The night air was still quite fresh. We walked briskly to her car and drove off. As we came to a patch of forest there was the dot on the I for this evening. Something bolted across the road in front of us. Maria stepped on the brakes. A fox! we both yelled in unison. Do you think a fox would cross the large plaza in front of the Muenchner Philharmonie building?

Notes from the 32nd North

Sent: Wednesday, 4 May 2011 ~ 3.52am

On time, at 2.00pm, on a Saturday, the plane touched down in Beirut. I was glad to get off it and walk on my two legs again. Had been sitting since the taxi picked me up at 4.30am – minus the run through the Frankfurt airport to change planes. But now I could sink into my husband's arms and car and recuperate. But before I sleep I would like to walk some more I told my husband. That would be great, he said, he wanted to show me something anyways, just the right tour. And it was a great tour. I had to climb a steep hill with many, many stairs leading to the top of the rocky coastline. Up there was the container with the offices overlooking a huge construction site. We stood out on a balcony about twenty metres or more above what was going to become the ground floor of this hotel. The night was warm enough to find the strong breeze from the Mediterranean pleasant. Below were a lot of lights for the workers to negotiate their work and walks safely across power lines, steel rods, wooden boards, and much more. This was the night shift. It was an impressive beehive of activity. I decided to take a picture of this tomorrow. Then, of course, I needed to climb down the steps to our adjacent hotel. My legs were in a slight tremor after that. But it was a nice exercise and a compliment to me to be taken to see a construction site at night. Not everybody gets such a privileged treatment. We shall be back tomorrow to take my pics.

And we did. It seemed to me that I was even higher up over the site today. My husband has always been a wonderful tour guide in such places. I have worn hard hats at other hotels to be. But this one was special since the office containers were way above the construction site. Wait here a minute, he instructed me. He stepped on two boards with a guard rail around as they went out into open air disappearing around the corner. Soon he came back.

Notwithstanding my acrophobia I followed him onto those boards as if I was fearless looking through the cracks to the ground twenty metres below. We have already a mock-up room, he said and opened sliding glass doors. Gratefully I stepped into the mock-up room, the one that was to become the typical hotel room. It had been nicely done, color coordinated, sparkling designs in the bathroom tiles and other luxury features. The huge bed was made up snow white and luscious all around. Now this bed, my husband said, has never been inaugurated, his eyes sparkling mischievously.

Notes from the 48th North

Sent: Sunday, 15 May 2011 ~ 9.48pm

A travel story remembered:

We are in a bus that is taking us out to the plane. What are you doing in Beirut? This I was asked by a Lebanese man going home. Pleasure or business? Must be business, he answers his own question before I can decide why I am going to Beirut. How did you decide? You are coming with a laptop, he says. Don't want to tell him about my book or that I want to see Byblos, or that I am going to Doha and Dubai and back to Beirut meeting journalists, photographers, and friends. Dubai feels like home still but at the same time there is also the thought that I don't live there anymore. Ring the doorbell at my friend's house in Dubai. Isolde! She is free on Sunday. We meet that day for a few hours that were squeezed out of a busy schedule. Thursday I am off to Canada for the summer, she said casually. Wasn't I lucky to come just in time to get those few hours time? Where is your son, she inquires. Both of our families are frequent travelers. Thus her question has merit. Oh, he is in Montreal, flew the same day I flew to Dubai. Actually, my whole family was in the air going in opposite directions. Got an email from him, I tell her proudly: I am in Montreal, everything is cool. Happy Mothers day Mama. Wow, he thought about that? Yes, great kid, isn't he? So goes the ritual of catching up between us.

Saturday we go by car to Abu Dhabi, meeting people for lunch: One for business and one couple for friendship dating back to Doha times, another couple for long term friendship dating back to Cairo times. We are all around one table. Was a very lively two hours. Let's do this again, where? Back in Dubai I meet my friend Caro during her Scottish dancing lesson. This is almost the only way to catch her. Joins us afterwards for a candle light dinner at the Golf

Club terrace. Goodbye, we say to each other. See whether you can stay a little longer next time, she adds. Yep, I agree! Tomorrow we will take a swim at our pool and then we are off to Qatar. Stay over night to meet friends, one couple dating back to Cairo, and one from Dubai. Next morning we are going back to Beirut. Did not even take my anti motion sickness patch off from behind my ear. Back in Beirut there is an email from our son: I am in Colorado at David's. Everything is cool. So, I take it, the whole family was again in the air at approximately the same day? In two days we are going back to Munich.

We arrive at 9.30pm. I am dashing ahead to buy some food for tomorrow's breakfast. Steven is waiting for the luggage. Ezio, our taxi driver, who has driven as back and forth between airport and home for about six years, since we lived in Cairo, is waiting, as always. I feel a strange regret being back, going home. It feels as if I am retreating from my world, where things are happening. Don't like the feeling, feel slightly sad. Isolde, you are back, Albert greets me the next morning in his store. He and his wife fill me in on the things I have missed. I am beginning to feel being back. It is Saturday. Is Steven here with you? he asks. Yes, but no, he had to go to the airport, somebody is changing planes and he has to have a meeting with him. Are you kidding, Albert exclaims. He will be back in a few hours. He has to because he went with my car! Indeed, in the afternoon he is back. Monday I have to go to London, he says, do you want to come with me? No thank you, my love, not for all the tea in China!

Monday morning the alarm of his mobile phone goes off. Dimly I register that he is getting up. Have a good trip and a good meeting and please bring back my car tonight, I say to him. After a while he comes back. I set the alarm two hours too early, he says. How come? Time on my mobile is UAE time, two hours ahead. Well, two more hours of sleep – REM sleep that is – for I had a dream: I was in an airport, talking to somebody, saying goodbye to somebody. Then I needed to go to my gate to fly off to somewhere. A friendly young man takes me to it. We are standing right at the gate and I realize we are in love with each other, but I need to go. I am not too sad, but he is very much though. Sad, I say to him, like it was not meant to be. Hopefully, Ann helps me to interpret this erotic dream staged in an airport! Where else?

Notes from the 48th North

Sent: Tuesday, 14 June 2011 ~ 5.47pm

When is he coming?

I was asked this once again in the self prescribed interval in the social meeting place of a provincial grocery store.

Friday.

How long is he going to stay this time?

For two weeks, well, with interruptions.

With interruptions again?

Where is he going?

Paris, for two days only.

And you are going with him again?

Don't know yet, maybe.

He invites you to come to Paris with him for two days and you hesitate?

Yes, give me a break!

I have been there before, I have even lived there once for a whole year, remember?

Yes, we remember, but Paris, Isolde!

Spotlight on a Stream of Consciousness

Well, maybe I am going, it is a quick like trip anyway.

Three pairs of eyes stare intensely into my face and then turn to look at each other.

Just a quick like trip to Paris – wow, Isolde?!

I can hear her think – nothing would be quick like for her – certainly not Paris. It is silent now – in a bit of incredulous atmosphere. Isolde, the ultimate snob! Rejecting a trip to Paris!

How can I make them understand where a nomadic person is coming from. It's Pierre, the clochard vs. Isolde, the snob. But they did their number on me. Come to think of it – it would be a great rendezvous with him on the Left Bank.

Notes from the 48th North

Sent: Tuesday, 21 June 2011 ~ 1.14pm

This was the case where a blind chicken found a mighty impressive corn. It was in the yard of a former cloister. The inhabitants have long since moved to other cloisters leaving this one to history. It is located on top of a hill right in front of Lake Chiemsee and the raggedy mountain Kampenwand – a very picturesque and famous part of the Bavarian Alps. The buildings are museums now, but the inn is very well and alive and serves wonderful food and awful non-alcoholic beer. The church, built during the Rococo period, is still spectacular with its twin towers. It is connected to another building of undefined use. My eyes were scanning the old walls. In a large niche I saw a large map saying something about 48. So I walked closer to read what it was about. It was true, the 48th North goes right through this place! I was, if you like, *standing on the 48th parallel*. I have found my friend and probably a part of my identity and my roots. See for yourself. I have attached proof. A strange feeling, isn't it?

Notes from the 48th North

Sent: Sunday, 26 June 2011 ~ 6.50am

Another rainy day – what to do with it on a Sunday? Taking a walk might be nice, to hear the drops on the corn leaves and the umbrella. That is, one umbrella for two, a very romantic thing to do – walking and singing in the rain. But my suppressed pleas for the sun to peak through were heard. The sky opened up, blue patches appeared, the color of the clouds gradually changed to white from gray. The wind diminished to a gentle breeze. By all means, lets go, now, or maybe again not for the next week. Let's walk through the forest and on to the 500-year-old saddle roof tower church, the one I attended a concert in a few weeks ago. People waived from closed cars as we walked. Did you recognize who it was? No matter – we are almost there. The farm right next to that church has a dog that usually roams the environment. Don't care, he said, lets go, I am with you. Well, no dog in sight anywhere. They must have taken him in (him? – dog is masculine in my language). After all, there are always visitors to this church on weekends. The view from its south side is just great. One can overlook the river valley, the city on the horizon, the Alps, if the clouds allow. But today it is fairly clear. Let's sit in that niche for a while. It protects you from the Easterlies and somewhat from the western onslaught of rain and wind. It is a corner for the tired wanderer or for lovers. I am both. It's a place to let the thoughts wander as well, drift off into far away places and fantasy land. It's the perfect place I let go, let my soul roam free. But strong pressure against my knee, a wet kiss on my hand, brings me back to reality pronto. Good grief, it is the wolf from The Wolf and the Seven Little Goats (Brothers Grimm)! Pull my hands in to my chest as far as possible. Well, it is the German Shepherd from this farm. He found us, wants to check us out. And more than anything he wants to play. I risk petting him. He responds by jumping up to my shoulders trying to lick my face. Have we met before and became friends? I push him down and try out what I know about dog etiquette: Setzen! He obeys and sits immediately. You are well trained, you went to dog school. He then flops down, turns on his back, puts his four legs into the air and exposes himself shamelessly and pleadingly. Gently.

I scratch and rub his belly. He loves it so much that he closes his eyes. Now that is ultimate trust. After a while my arm starts to get tired. I am tired, I tell the nameless dog. He stands up, jumps up on me and tries to lick my face again. No, I yell, you don't need to thank me, you are welcome. He understands my language and leaves just as suddenly as he had appeared.

How is that for a Sunday afternoon?

Notes from the 48th North

Sent: Sunday, 3 July 2011 ~ 9.08am

It is 4.30am Let's rise and shine and drive to the airport. Sunday morning it should only take about an hour. Usually it is a pleasant drive, with crisp, clean air, almost silence, dew, and the light of the sun appearing ever so faintly indicating the turning of the Earth.

And so it is. Driving back out of the airport I am now alone in the car. That peaceful bliss lasts only till I reach my favorite stop. It is a brand new, pleasantly clean, and inviting store at the first service station outside of the airport area. Only the woman working there is present. She is still setting up stuff. Please get me one of those miserable croissants, I demand grouchily. She looks up and grins at me. Don't feel like grinning, but I explain: Did you also get up at 4.30 today? I ask her with challenge in my voice. No, she answers still with her stupidly friendly grin. I got up a 4.00, I have to be here to open this shop at 6.00am and I have two dogs to take care of before I leave.

Well, that's voluntary, I snap. Sorry, I am in an inexplicably bad mood. Have a good day and a good drive now anyways, she says pleasantly. I make an effort to undo what I have done: And you have a good day. I turn around with the miserable croissant in my hand and look directly into the grinning face of a man. Is today the annual grin-day?

Actually this croissant is crispy, not bad, not like rubber, just pleasant. Perhaps I am actually at Charles De Gaulle? Let's get out of here, back on the road. I am doing 110 to 120, my angry speed on a two lane highway. And that jerk of a FIAT driver is passing me up in a no passing zone. Who do you think you are to overtake my Passat? Do you know about FIAT? – Fix It Again Toni! So there. And you, with your rinky dink small scale Mercedes, are you on dope passing me and the Fix It Again Toni? Perhaps you are just an anti-social personality disorder and too ignorant to know traffic laws and dangers. But probably you are all of the above. Go on then you all. I will turn on my music, so there! Okay, I need to slow down, I am coming into Erding ... and there they are both of them: Rinky dink small scale and Fix It Again Tony! Now we are all happy together again, you want-to-be-Vettels. You both are turning in both directions. That's good, I was about to honk and tell you to get out of my way, for today I am not a well balanced character. The sun is not coming up, but the rain is. It is coming out of a gray sky, it will rain all day and it is only sixteen degrees. No lazy-hazy day of summer, but cold-turn-on-the-heating-summer. Who put those horses out on the pasture so early in the morning, in the rain? They graze peacefully, seemingly undisturbed and the cows down the country road a ways as well. It is getting better, the world looks calmer. I am home. Send an SMS I am home, I am okay. The telephone rings: Thanks for the SMS, thanks for getting up so early to take me to the airport. You are welcome, I would not want to miss the time with you. Have a pleasant trip now and say hello to the sun.

Notes from the 48th North

Sent: Friday, 8 July 2011 ~ 5.46pm

I had given up on it, giving in to my frustration. And I have tried repeatedly, have asked computer freaks, e-bay savvy customers and husbands and sons. To no avail – until two days ago. I tried to refill my credit on Skype for phone activities. Again, after "you are almost there" payment was rejected. I must have changed, for this time I wanted to know it! I called Hans, my reliable IT man, who always shows up almost promptly, when I have a problem. He tried ... and failed ... repeatedly. Finally, he suggested to call my bank re my credit card. Is there something wrong with it when she smells cyberspace? Yes, the voice on the telephone bank call center answered. You have to specially register nowadays with them, specially for internet, PayPal and such use. Could you have let me know that sooner, dear bank? So, Hans asked, shall we do it? You, bet, can you do it? If I have to. Poor Hans has a bit of a problem with my keyboard from Dubai because it also has Arabic letters and numbers on it. Although, he has gone online to take it should I ever get rid of it! But back to the issue. First one has to think up a sentence that has to pop up every time I start the confusing attempt to pay anything via PayPal or its competition. Next you will get about eight questions offered of which you have to select and answer four. And it should be four with answers you can remember. Next you need a user name which, of course, you need to remember. Hans! I don't need PayPal in my life. Let's get out of it. I will live some other way! He laughs without compassion for me, but in a knowing way. Next, you need a password. No, Hans, no, nobody is going to use this wicked system. We won't ever stay ahead of cyberspace crime and abuse for long anyways. We do, he reassures me, if it becomes a tight race again, we just add another sentence to answer and to remember the answer. Okay, I will write them all down and stick them on my credit card. Problem solved!

Calm down and resign to the realities of modern life. This will get worse, as it does so already all the time and in relative silence.

In future I will have more and more work, Hans says with a grin of satisfaction.

Well, we did figure that one out, didn't we? They won't get ahead of me, I wrote everything down in my travel diary a good friend of mine once gave me.

Notes from the 48th North

Sent: Sunday, 10 July 2011 ~ 5.49pm

It was to be a party of a different kind. This village is located on top of a hill and her house, my walking partner's, is on a hill on top of the hill. It has got a most beautiful panorama view over the two-river-valley.

The horizon is formed either by the Alps or haziness. With that as a background she had set the tables and backless benches into the grass, beer garden style. Umbrellas protected us from the July sun, but not for long. For the view to the west was also unhindered.

There the sky had started to darken and moved closer covering the sun. A light wind cooled the guests and the heated discussions about females playing soccer, as if that was a question of monumental importance (not to worry, guys, Germany lost the eleven metre shoot out, and they are out).

After another thirty minutes the sky, not just the horizon anymore, was so dark that the strings of party lights came on. Little Cindy crawled under a bench and spread her four legs for cooling in the grass.

For almost 180 degrees there was a threatening wall of blue-gray-black. It lit up rose, orange, or bright white-red-orange every few seconds. Enormous snakes of lightening flickered across the sky or straight down.

A distant rumble went on continuously. At the first drop of rain, no, before that, at the first real thunder the women grab the bottles, the glasses, and tried to remember which belonged to whom.

The men lifted up the tables and benches and ran into the soccer semi-public viewing cottage of the son of the house. Then somebody pointed east and shouted: There is another one over there, look at the lightening! That makes 270 degrees of thunderstorms. It was a spectacular show and a party of a different kind. Thank you, happy birthday, dear.

Notes from the 48th North

Sent: Wednesday, 13 July ~ 11.05am

Unfortunately I did not see it. I read it in the Sueddeutsche Zeitung, the Munich daily, I believed it fully. For they have humor (of sorts) and they are casual and contrary, as needed. There is this fountain in front of city hall. It has a wide basin and in the middle is a column rising up. On top of that are three (stone) fish – yes, you guessed it – it is called the Fish Fountain. It's the fountain where we used to meet our dates. It is the fountain where people rest, sit on, play music, read a book, have lunch, and still meet a date. Well, yesterday there was a trout swimming in that basin. So the Munich daily reported. Actually it was not swimming around, just floating, floating completely motionless. Probably she was checking out her new environment in disbelief. It was a warm day. That water might have been too warm for her. She needs the colder waters of the creeks coming down from the Bavarian Alps. They are very cold! The police and the firefighters tried their best to catch the slippery, elegant, dashing-about-trout to no avail. Finally, the Munich Zoo people had to come with special equipment. She is now in her new and suitable home in said zoo and recovers from her trauma. Gosh, what a fishy story! I will report tomorrow from the reaction of the animal rightists. – Tja, those were the days in Berkeley, in the Bay Area, and behind the Berkeley Hills when they put laundry soap into those fountains. It was harmless! It was la bella fontana only! I saw it with my own eyes. It was not a fishy story at all.

Spotlight on a Stream of Consciousness

Notes from the 48th North

Sent: Thursday, 14 July 2011 ~ 3.33pm

You are in Munich – until mid August? Of course, I will come. Meet where? What place is that, I don't seem to have heard of it, let alone been there? Okay, I will find it. How come you can introduce me to a new art gallery, a restaurant – cafe mixture in it – in my city? You are Viennese, you are causing me anxiety. Am I becoming a stranger in my city of origin, my city of coming of age? I'll be there before you, I'll find it blindly. Servus, darling, it has been two years! Why so long?

You look the same, ageless and smooth. How and where have you been? What did you do for four weeks in Paris? Did we not want to go together next time around? No, I did not need time out, too, I needed to meander through Paris with you, trying on crazy hats and shoes and the whole haute couture.

For two and one half hours we talked trying to catch up and reconnect our lives. But then, despite of the two years it did not feel at all as if we had been disconnected. She is one of those rare people who can stay emotionally close over time and distance. It felt like we simply picked up where we had left off – where actually was it? – could it have been Cairo? No, we have met in Munich since then? Good grief, we all have to slow down a little. And then, for one hour we meandered through Munich. It was a rainy, windy, and cold day for July. We did not notice, did not care, there was so much to share, to laugh about, some to regret, some to support for each of us. Share our lives. How is Conrad? she asked. Now that is a good idea, shall we meet in Berlin next time?

What made this reunion such a pleasure? For me it is being understood, being accepted as is, sharing the ups and downs of life, it is as therapeutic as genuine friendship can be, it is the inner connectedness, no need to pretend and the lasting through time, the trust, the familiarity – twenty years we go back and counting, I am sure. Yeah, that's the other point: We have a history together. Two weekends from now the four of us intend to enjoy a night on the town. Then she will go back to Vienna and I will most likely go to Beirut and the Emirates. Vienna seems to be further away than the Emirates, but no less close for sure. The emotional connectedness is what helps to sustain emotionally healthy life. Homo sapiens is a social animal.

Notes from the 48th North

Sent: Friday, 22 July 2011 ~ 8.01am

Finally, I found the answer to all the riddles – about the beauty of a kiss. Kissing is romantic, telling, gives you ideas, and makes you feel good. And that's just it! Now I know why the lift. Thanks to the research report of my beloved *Prevention* Magazine (August 2011, pg 19, Rodale Press) I want you to know this: Male saliva contains testosterone and a lingering kiss is a reliable delivery system. And – in both sexes kissing floods the bloodstream with dopamine which – let that sink in – stimulates the same part of the brain as cocaine does. Now don't get any funny ideas! And – it says that heart health is a beneficiary of kissing as the activity reduces cholesterol in men and women. Now I loved kissing for ever but now I don't know. Let's see whether we can replicate this study empirically. Enjoy!

Notes from the 48th North

Sent: Sunday, 31 July 2011 ~ 11.50pm

It almost alarmed me! Have I lost my connection, the grip on my anchor all these years, on my city of origin? Of course, this is a bit over the top because the answer is NO with very slight amendments. Nonetheless, how come that my friend, native to Vienna, who no longer lives in Munich but, well, in Vienna, can show me new places in my own town? Goes to show you that life is dynamic, that places move on, that I don't stroll through Munich often enough. I mean, ask me about Dubai, Doha or Cairo and I have answers. Well, on Wednesday I intend to start implementing my resolve to change the situation. And then, when I come to Vienna I will relax. You are telling me!

Notes from the 48th North

Sent: Thursday, 18 August 2011 ~ 5.54pm

It is difficult to write this, but it should be written. It is my tribute to an unusual friendship. I don't know when she saw me the first time. My memory of her starts when I was about ten years old. Almost every Saturday I helped her with her work as custodian of the church. I handed her bunches of flowers when she stood up on the altar. I remember her nine months pregnant in that situation. I pushed her first child in a pram so that she could work. She has taken me into the church choir as she was the organist for probably more than thirty years. She has taught me the rudiments of music theory. She has taught and exercised with her children's choir the mass from Hayden. I still can sing bits and pieces from it. Later as an adult I made sure I visited her when I came home from somewhere in the world. She was one of very few that asked how I felt having to live in the foreign land of America. In the last two years I could visit her more often as I lived in the same village again. You have been so many places and have learned so much – that's what she said to me just a few months ago – I have not been anywhere and have not learned a lot. I agreed with the former but not with the latter. She has survived a horrendous war, she has raised five children afterwards, she has lost one grandchild by suicide. She handled it all with grace and without ever yelling. I have never heard her yell. Lately she was my best source of information about my own family during the times I had not been born yet. It pleased her that I would attempt to write a book about one of them. Come again, she said every time I left. Last Tuesday I visited her in the hospital. She had stumbled at home and broken her upper thigh bone. When I entered her room she greeted me by saying she had "been waiting" for me. What made for this unusual connection between us. I don't know really. For me, she just was so pleasant a person to be with, so lively, so thinking. Just in the past year she had told me what she really felt about the catholic church and her teachings. I was very surprised that she had ever questioned her faith, and, more so, that she would tell me about it.

I have spoken to four of her five children yesterday – in the same house. She was not there anymore. She will never be in it again. Her daughter described her mother's last hours in intensive care. From that I conclude that she had mastered her death with the same determination she had mastered a challenging life. She apparently tore off her oxygen mask and through it with vigor from her declaring that she has had enough. Yet, her daughter said that she died peacefully and when she determined it should be. Regina, it was well worth to have enjoyed her friendship, every bit of it. If there is a heaven she must be in it.

Notes from the 48th North

Sent: Thursday, 25 August 2011 ~ 8.07pm

These are the last lazy, hazy summer days of this mostly rained out season. To lure us into looking forward to next summer this one is showing us what it could have been. The days are above the desired 30C mark, quite above. And finally, my fellow citizens here acknowledge my foreign life. At least once a day I am asked: Is it warm enough for you now? Yes, it is just beginning to get there, during the day, that is. At night it is another story as this is a country that believes in technology, to be sure, but not in ACs for private homes. So at night, yeah we are hot and uncomfortable and whine for the return of the rainy days. Beautiful, spectacular, and often disastrous thunderstorms mercifully cool down the earth around us. But not enough to cool us down all together. We can't sleep as judged by the lights on at night and by learning from heated stories about insomnia when we meet during the day.

I have my own methods to cope, like sitting at my computer and writing this. But having shingles and the resulting discomfort also drives me out of bed ... and out into the dew soaked grass, like this night. It is completely still, not even the slightest rustling in the nut tree. I took my binoculars with me being hard put to set up my telescope at night. Starry, starry night, I am thinking all the time – you know – Vincent van Gogh? It is also an unusually dark night, can't understand why. I am gazing with and without binoculars into the night sky. It is so brilliant, so sparkling, so overwhelmingly star sparkled all earthen problems seem insignificant for the moment, including shingles pains. And my beloved Milky Way is quite visibly there. It still exists. I have not seen it in a long while as the places are lit up too much, usually. I am thinking what my friends at the southern hemisphere see in their night sky. Can't remember at all what the Sydney night sky looked like.

Another summer subject on my mind is the summer in Munich and the visitors that come along with the warm season. Delightfully, it brought my friend from Vienna. She would not want to be named and I am unable to assign her another name. By coincident she and her family had reason to spend the summer in Munich which was a special treat for us both. We used it well. We visited new restaurants, new arcades, new exhibitions in former old places that we knew. We talked the hours away, we meandered through the city, laughing, talking, stopping and going. Our time together was so invigorating and challenging that shopping was not an issue for us. She told me about her time in Paris and I told her about Dubai, Doha, and Beirut. We compared our same age sons, formerly schoolmates. You are making me feel better, she said. Thank you, you are challenging my rationales. She came to the farm to spend the night, her husband picking her up the next day. Him I had met last time in our place in Cairo which dates back at least eight years. And then the summer was over.

That was it then. Thank you for so refreshing a time, so uplifting (I agree, no other lifting is necessary anywhere), so rejuvenating, so healing. Oh, and one more thing, she sent an SMS. Son will come by one more time on his way back from Vienna to Munich. Can you fill his buckets one more time with your apples and plumbs? They are so delicious. Can't buy them in stores. Well, I had a most interesting two hours with him and his charming, engaging Austrian ways. He told me vividly about his Ersatz time in a home for the handicapped in lieu of serving time in the Austrian army. He talked about his time with autistic teens and adults. He told me things about them that I had not known. And he is cavalier, never overlooking my empty glass. Thank you all, who cares about the rain?

My neighbor happened to be over for a chat. I just can hear him talking to his wife about Isolde: Husband not home and she gets visited by a twenty-six-year-old. Steven howled with laughter when I told him about my possibly damaged reputation. And I also tell him about the heap of brochures and maps my friend has left on our living room table. Planning to visit Vienna come theater season.

Thank you! I hope next year's summer wind brings my visitors back. So when is one of you coming by? My door is always open.

Notes from the 22nd North

Sent: Wednesday, 7 September 2011 ~ 5.02am

It was all peaceful around me. Only the splashing of the water and the delightful screeching of small children reached my ears as they jumped into the pool. I was reading Arabic short stories from a Beirut born author. Sometimes I apparently dozed off as I found my book lying beside me and out of my hands. Peace and bliss. A voice right next to me made me open my eyes. There stood a man and said: I am giving you this watch. He put it on my blanket by my feet. It did not take me more than a few seconds to understand what he meant. He wanted me to guard his wrist watch while he swam with his four friends, all of them watching me. Of course I will keep an eye on your 3000 dollar watch. Any time! Is it your youthful innocence or the fact that I am not a thief that makes me so trustworthy? My honor! I just will be a little late for the date with my husband. It is not every day that I am trusted to that magnitude by a complete stranger.

Notes from the 32nd North

Sent: Saturday, 10 September 2011 ~ 3.32am

Did you notice? I was confused. The 22nd North would have put me in the vicinity of Cairo. Perhaps it was wishful thinking? No, I am here at the 32nd North. And soon I hope to be at the 48th North. Temperatures will change along with latitude from 30C to 20C and below. I shall not complain for being cool as well as keeping my cool each has its merit. Until then ...

Notes from the 48th North

Sent: Tuesday, 4 October 2011 ~ 7.59am

He called at 11.00pm and my adrenalin level shot up in anticipation. You, is it really you? You never call, cyberspace is your line of communication, if at all. My aunt died. It took me three times asking to comprehend what he had said.

You were my sister-in-law until you became more *sis* than *in law*. I started out in California in your and your husband's apartment.

We talked a lot about your work as counselor at juvenile hall. I admired you for your guts. I visited you in San Jose after your divorce. We talked it out, we tried to heal your wounds. We went on a pleasure drive to Santa Cruz, we dined and laughed. You shared with me about your la vie d'amour. You sent me so many great videos after I had moved back to Europe to keep me supplied with the originals. You were not mad at me for taking your brother away with me. You held my baby son, you loved him and he loved you. You had this great voice that I could never hear enough of. You never made an issue of it. Rather, you played down. You visited us in Munich. You drove my car at high speed over a German autobahn as if you had done it many times before. We went to Chiemsee, took a boat to the island with the castle. It was the first castle for you. We went to Neuschwanstein and walked up to that castle. Well, you were not born a mountaineer. You read *Far Away from the Brewery* and had so kind things to say about your brother and me in terms of our relationship and life. You said things that even I had not considered myself. So why did you leave us so early and so unexpectedly? And you left the way you lived, quiet, undisturbing, unobtrusive, not causing any commotions. You did it alone in your apartment, over a weekend. It was Monday morning when people noticed that you were not there. Your brother will come to put you to rest. And I will come one of these days again to your place, to the land that was yours and became mine eventually. And I will put into California earth what was the last thing you told me you loved from me: My News from the 48th North. That is a promise, sis.

Notes from the 48th North

Sent: Tuesday, 15 November 2011 ~ 7.52am

At the crack of a winterish dawn we were on our way to the airport. Everything was frosted over white. It looked so pretty, calming, and romantic and thus almost mocked the real task at hand – drop him off at the airport and change to a solo life for a while, again. Up on the slippery bridge a light wavered back and forth. Watch out, there must be a person walking. Sure enough! That's that hobo, what is he doing here at this time and in this frosted over world? Oh, and look, in front of us is the salt truck, lets pass him up and drive on unsalted road.

Turning the car into the exit road, on my way home, the first red sun rays peeked over the horizon. They were kind to my mood and turned everything pink. Even the Kondenzstreifen, painted into the sky by a few planes, were pink. Frosty pink trees, meadows, skylines of patches of forest worked on my romantic soul. I could not help but to acknowledge the beauty of nature despite my somber mood. I stopped at the service station next to the airport as I usually do. My tristess mood was right at the surface of my mood scala. Pulling away to go on the highway I switched the radio to "Bayern Klassik". I need Beethoven's 8th. It fit my mood, has done the trick before. But no, instead I heard "My almost Lover", yeah, that might do it, too. I stopped two more times to take pictures of that therapeutic morning scenery. Everything looked so mysterious. Thank you, I gradually felt my down mood get into place where it belonged.

I was almost home, drove through the still sleepy village. Only one man walked on the sidewalk. By golly, this is my sporty neighbor. He waved; I pulled into our driveway, waiting for him to approach. Isolde, what are you doing, where have you been at this time? I was at the airport, where else? You been jogging – at this time? No, just got myself a newspaper. Jogging later? Power walk? You bet! I was home and ready.

Notes from the 48th North

Sent: Wednesday, 7 December 2011 ~ 5.50pm

It was another one of those insomnia-ridden nights. But this had its merits. It was a very stormy night. Stepping out onto the balcony, I was surprised to see so few clouds that the stars had enough windows to show themselves in the full beauty of a cold winter night.

They seemed to race across the sky until they went behind a cloud. A very nice visual illusion, for it is the racing clouds that make the stars appear to fly like a lot of satellites. Visual illusions were my favorite subject within Neuropsychology back then in Washington, DC when I was an undergraduate.

But I stepped back inside quickly for fear that the storm might chill me down to the bone. Inside, when I keep still, I usually enjoy the music of the high winds. Sometimes they howl high-pitched, reminding me of the coyotes in the Santa Monica Mountains in California. I loved to hear them at night. And sometimes the winds thunder and bring wonderful pictures to my mind from wonderful days at the Pacific beaches of Northern California. Never will I forget the sound of those mighty waves crashing onto shore. My partner, born next to the stormy surf of the Pacific Northwest, was teaching me to always keep one eye out over the ocean lest you are surprised and drowned by one big one. When I was standing with him on Bondi beach in Australia looking into the Pacific from the other side I was still very green to ocean matters. But Bavaria is not a maritime threat by any means. Yet, this storm brought all the memories back. I loved the sound of it. After all I was safely inside. Still, I missed his hand crawling over to mine and holding it reassuringly. Yesterday evening I was watching Don Giovanni from the Milano Scala with Anna Netrebko mostly to try to find out why one of my friends favors this opera. My apologies to Mozart and my friend, I prefer the music of this storm.

Notes from the 48th North

Sent: Sunday, 18 December 2011 ~ 2.33am
MISTLETOE *by Walter de la Mare*
Sitting under the mistletoe

(Pale-green fairy mistletoe), One last candle burning low, All the sleepy dancers gone, Just one candle burning on, Shadows lurking everywhere:

Someone came, and kissed me there. Tired I was, my head would go Nodding under the mistletoe

(Pale-green, fairy mistletoe),

No footsteps came, no voice, but only, Just as I sat there, sleepy, lonely,

Stooped in the still and shadowy air

Lips unseen – and kissed me there.

I wish you a Merry Christmas and a kiss under that mistletoe,

Love,

Isolde

Notes from the 48th North

Sent: Tuesday, 20 December 2011 ~ 1.53pm

Off and on it snowed all day. And in darkness it added another dimension to winter with those white flakes drifting down silently. I felt cozy indoors. But there was the movie, the classic of mystery that I needed to watch again. That got me away from the window. Have you seen *The Third Man*? That movie got under my skin the first time I saw it, and it did the same again tonight. Graham Green had selected the best location for his story by placing it into Vienna. Vienna, the great metropolis and with the great history of the Austrian – Hungarian Danube Monarchy (Oesterreichisch-Ungarische Donau Monarchy). It was destroyed by a terrible war. It was in shambles and in rubble. Nothing, seemingly, was left of its former glory. It was divided into an American, French, a Russian, and a British section. That city is the real hero of that movie, before Harry Lyme. Life in those post-war times was very difficult for the Viennese. It was a time where one had to be innovative to make it physically as well as mentally. The whole story was filmed in a rainy city. And the music surely was Viennese, not the dream of a Johann Strauss waltz, but sad and lost. It masterfully conveyed the life in a destroyed city. But it seems like the citizens tricked the occupiers with the skills they seem to have in their genes – to take life casually and enjoy. The actor Paul Hoerbiger, a man from a Viennese actors' dynasty had it put into his script: *Get out of here, or I forget my Viennese charm!*

Probably I feel a little like the essence of this story. I am native, I am home, but the home and I are not the same from before anymore. Strangely enough, today I feel more mixed than usually, to say the least. I feel Christmas-like, enjoy the snow, but want to be elsewhere where it is so warm that I need only one skimpy layer of clothes. I stomped through Munich the other day and felt it to be my city, but from before, not from now. We are going to Dubai for a vacation, Maxl said to me yesterday. I explained and talked to help him enjoy it when there. Felt like I was talking about my home, but not from now, from before.

The Third Man, besides being just a great story, artistic almost, it speaks to me somehow. And it screams "international", that the city was for sure, still is, and the movie had two grand actors in it, one from the US and one a native Viennese.

Do you know what I mean?

Notes from the 48th North

Sent: Saturday, 14 January 2012 ~ 5.04am

It was a strong winter storm with rain, snow, and, well, very strong winds. They blew through our clothing and aired us out. Cindy's white hair and little ears were whipped about. She quit barking and had turned her head downwind. But she had a great time sniffing out every mouse hole and every ditch. She did not even limp anymore. Her arthritis seemed also to be blown away. The ten year old white, long-haired Schnauzer mutt lady was fine. We went through the forest to get out of the wind. Unfortunately, we frightened two deer. They jumped up and ran across our path. Today, Cindy was not on a leash. And the old lady showed us what old age means when things are exciting. She tore after the two far jumping deer as if she had a chance to catch them. The shouting and calling of her master walking next to me she ignored. We only saw two white, stubby little legs in a blurred way. Panting she waited for us a little down the path. She looked at us with a wildly going tail. So much for old age, her eyes flashed at us. It was an uplifting experience for all involved and uninvolved.

I went to the doctor. Doc, constantly people are talking about all the activities they have to stop as soon as they are getting older, and they do mean old like past forty! Constantly there are warnings around me. What's to it? The mother of my pharmacist is eighty two and goes jogging a few times a week. What's to come? Get on the bike, Isolde, let us draw some blood and all. Haven't done this in two years, right? Yep. After that we know about the state of health in terms of your sporty activities. Now then, you can keep going, no restrictions in your sports. Even snow shoveling is fine. Oh, shucks, doctor, I thought this is out from thirty on up! Get out a here! Gladly! It was an uplifting experience.

I watched that movie the other day: *The Man in the Iron Mask*. It was about the French queen, apparently the mother of Luis XIV. Don't know whether there is any truth to it. In the movie she was the mother of twins (both played by Leonardo di Caprio). One was hidden away in a prison with an iron mask over his head to hide his face – done to him by his twin brother as he wanted to be the king. Anyway, there was d'Artangon? Him, from *The Three Musketeers* by Alexandre Dumas? And there they came – Artos first ... all three. They had retired from their wild duties. They have aged, they were old Musketeers now. Their looks told of years gone by. Nothing else had aged, not their spirit, not their vitality and *Sturm und Drang*, their determination, their defiance of death. They fought like the dickens still. They defied the effects of age, it just was not an issue. Their youthful spirit was remarkable, and, of course, made them subdue the enemy of the second twin, i.e. the *The Man in the Iron Mask* (who became Luis XIV). I did not know that there was a continuation of *The Three Musketeers*. Although I have no idea who wrote *The Man in the Iron Mask*. Anyway, it was another uplifting experience.

Notes from the 48th North

Sent: Sunday, 5 Feb 2012 ~ 9.05am

The day started innocently enough. The sunrise featured pink and then orange colors. The leafless walnut tree looked like an ink drawing against that sky. The air was crystal clear providing a view into the Alps. Like the whole last week, I quickly stepped out the door to read the thermometer: – 14C, and that is measured directly on the wall of the house. I added three degrees to get the approximate temperature measured further out and twenty-centimetre above the frozen earth. Jumped back in, slammed the front door shut, fixed breakfast with hot tea. I turned on the TV with the info of the winter sport areas in Bavaria and in Austria. With a low key voice the speaker announced: Hintertux Glacier with -23C, Zillertal only -20C. Well, neither is a good temperature to ski. Muscles are hard to warm up. Although as a kid we did not care, we never knew the temperature outdoors. It was either freezing fingers and toes, or not.

Brave walking partner I have. She came with me for our power walk. We tried to keep our mouths closed and breathe through the nose. Now my skin inside the nose is bloody. My brother tried to convince me that I should stay indoors. Perhaps I should, but this frozen world and frozen, clear air is a delightful experience, and, of course, it makes you feel like being a tough girl. People were curling on the frozen pond behind the forest. Isolde, do you want a Stamperl Schnapps? Yes, please! I drank it even though I know better.

At night one can see the Milky Way and so many stars. But the cold is even worse and does not allow for a lengthy viewing. How then did we do it way back when we walked for twenty minutes along a path, at least where we thought the path must be, at pitch dark night, in the State of Salzburg, after a whole day of ski lessons. We were invited from a local family to taste their Blueberry Schnaps. When we stumbled back to the village and our hotel, a few hours later, we were feeling warm. Was it really -20C? Sure did not feel like it. Don't kiss me on my lips on the way back! Too cold!

Notes from the 48th North

Sent: February 2012

You were at the airport when your son and I returned from Australia. That's when we met for the first time. It was a difficult beginning for us, wasn't it? But in time we began to understand each other, even like each other despite our differences. When you finally one time called me your daughter our acceptance was complete. We shared many interests. One certainly was our love for traveling. When you were young you had to move a lot, but I beat you to it and got your full admiration for it. But after retirement your time came. You and your husband dared to fly halfway around the world and came to see us in Istanbul. Next you spent one summer with us in Munich. And you came twice, all by yourself, to see us in Cairo. And you flew from there to Ethiopia! Even I would have been scared to do that. You where a mover and shaker, and a rebel all your life. You were the kind of person born before their time. Your world was not quite ready for you. I hope you now have the peace that was often elusive to you when you were young.

You did not know that your daughter preceded you to the world that the Indians called the eternal hunting grounds. And you spoke a little bit of their language, didn't you? Don't worry, it lives on in your children and grandchildren. The ashes of your daughter will accompany you on this last trip of yours. We knew that you were preparing for departure. So it is not a shock to me. Instead, sadness about your leaving has more room to take place. You were not easy, you were challenging, and sometimes without compromise. Nonetheless, you were the right mother-in-law for me.

So please take my Notes with you. I promised your daughter to put them into the earth she is buried in. Just never thought you would be the messenger.

Notes from the 48th North

Sent: Friday, 16 March 2012 ~ 11.00am

Yesterday I drove to the airport to send somebody off to California. Today I drove to the airport to send two off to Berlin. They all left. I was doing very well during the day. People came by, the day was warm, no jacket, birds singing like there was a competition. The evening following what the day promised: beautiful sunset, still warm, still a joint venture bird concert. But there was nobody, no person, no laughter, no talk, no loved ones, or friends. I thought I was a master at both being left and leaving myself. But now I am just a little heap of depression and sad feelings.

Hope I can pick somebody up on Monday. And it's the plan that he will leave on Tuesday early. Back to the airport. Weird how the most soothing, tranquil atmosphere can invite melancholy and depression. Seems like a paradox, should be. But then I know it isn't. You know that song 'Melancholy in September'? It was in Italy, Finale Ligure, at the beach. Felt just the same feeling for seemingly no reason then. Came and went. So will this.

Notes from the 48th North

Sent: Monday, 26 March 2012 ~ 5.31pm

We will separate, move away into opposite directions, into different countries and continents but we have Facebook. It will soften the blow. It was our attempt to cope with the pain of losing each other, ending a stretch of life together and going our separate ways. And it did work to a degree. There they popped up on Facebook, my friends and me in our different locations. We had daily contact, instant contact if needed. This way I stayed connected with most of them for the last three years. I still love to read the triviality as it gives me the illusion that we are not as separated as we could be, and that our time together has not ended completely. And, yes, of course, when it is necessary, email, and wonderful Skype are keeping the friendships going. I am ever so grateful to modern electronics.

But Facebook is gradually getting me to rethink my use of them. My IT man has been on my case for ever to demonstrate to me how he lives and has friendships without Facebook use. You would have to pay me a lot of money before I join Facebook, he exclaims time and again while he is running my computer through his virus check. What is his reasoning for such dislike? First you catch all kinds of viruses and Trojans. And I don't need 248 friends. I have one or two close ones. Get out of it, Isolde. Those that are really interested in you will use email and Skype. He was really on my case this time. I had called him because I could not sign myself out of Facebook. No matter how many times I clicked the sign out thing it came back. Perhaps those two of my friends that were permanently shown as being on Facebook line also were unable to sign out and just had given up on it? Well, Hermann can get into my computer from his office if I click it so. I watched him try. That's not possible, how can that be ... I heard him say for the better part of an hour. At the end he got me signed out at the price of having to type in scrambled words to sign in again. And there was no other way now! Perhaps if you don't want to stay on Facebook forever, 24/7, they make it so difficult for you to sign in again that you give up and stay on. So he suggested in an "of course" tone. Some of those scrambled words were not even readable. Why, Facebook has only one purpose for its existence, he says, they sell commercial space. For that they need you online. I know he is right, but I cannot bring myself to close out my Facebook, close out my friends. But it might come to that. He tried again: Why else would Facebook need storage space as large as six soccer fields? There is a lot of info stored you cannot take back, he says. Well, perhaps I am saved from my conflict should I not be able to close out Facebook all together. I am going to have to stay tuned. So far, I can get in and out of Facebook on Mozilla. Holding my breath ...

Notes from the 48th North

Sent: Tuesday, 3 April 2012 ~ 3.36pm

This is the second night I am tossing and turning still at midnight. Can't sleep, can't relax. A short sentence from my friend that came across cyberspace is getting around in my head like a windmill. This night I have given up. I know this needs to be written down. So here I am trying to put into words what the matter is without being polemic, overly romantic, or dramatic. Just dealing with the issue, if I can determine the predicament.

I have not received your Notes for a while, she wrote. Let's Skype on Monday 12.00am my time. Searching my lousy memory I knew that I had not forgotten to send them to her, not ever. Not her! For she is one born at so different a place than me, from so different a background. When our paths met we felt the vibes of an inner connection almost immediately. She verbalized that too: There is a special bond between us, she said one day. She is also one of those that can stay close over distance and time. I have no doubt that we still will Skype many years from now. And there is another statement that another friend from a distant land and so foreign a background has sent to me after my last Notes: Friends are those that do not need to be reminded of our existence. How true! It made me think, again, of all those that left my life when I moved away. They were also close friends. With some the connection lasted for a while. But I wonder now where they are, how they are, what they have done since we separated. I would like to know. Oblivion has swallowed them up. We had shared our fears and pains, our desires and hopes, and we could let our souls hang free when together. But apparently they did not see sense in staying connected when the prospects of ever living close again where minimal. Now they feel like doors have closed to segments of my life. They once were real in my life, and wonderful friends; now they feel like dreams, unreal, like they kept part of my history to themselves. I am missing something about myself without them.

Then there was the most down-to-earth reaction to one of my recent Notes: Come and see me, if you feel lonesome! Bless her heart! Yes, I agree, let's continue, or perhaps revitalize, what we once did, get together and enjoy just that. It has been three years. I shall leave on Wednesday.

And then: Thank you for including me in your circle. That felt so nice in my heart for she also stays close over time and distance. Once we have spent four intense years together, grew together and grew closer, too. I am happy that this door stayed open, eight years after my departure. Thank you, let's keep it this way. How could it possibly close after what we have shared?

So what keeps us losing or staying connected to each other? Certainly the compatibility of two personalities are the crux of the matter, life philosophies shared, experiences shared, histories lived through together. What about the desire to keep a relationship going in the absence of sharing space? Or does the pain of separation with slim hopes of reversing, the inability to see sense in a long distance connection, or to see still a benefit, make some close the door? The here and now issue is an issue for some? And what about the ease of communicating? Curiously, the friends I have lost are mostly from the age of letters written on paper and mailed. Except two! One of those two once, years ago, exclaimed: Will we ever see each other again? Yes, we do with ease if we choose so.

The thought that technology could have a hand in my living friendships of today does not settle comfortably with me. But by all means, it is easy to email and Skype!

Feeling calm now. Thanks for listening.

Notes from the 48th North

Sent: Sunday, 8 April 2012 ~ 2.32am

Time to clean and store away winter boots for the summer. Time to exchange the winter tires for summer easier-going tires. All done. Since then it got slowly colder and wetter. Artic cold air will move in for the Easter holidays, bringing along some rain and snow. Really? Indeed! Today, Easter Sunday morning, when the shutters moved up it all was covered in snow and still coming down. No way will I pull out my boots again. This is almost three weeks into Spring and I am more than ready for warm weather. And in addition, I am packing to go to the French Riviera a few latitudes less than 48. I am thinking summer, warm, beach and Mediterranean. But I have to pick up my schoolmate as I agreed to go to Easter Mass this morning with her to the big cathedral. It's the music, Isolde, she used as an argument to get me to come along. I give in, pull out my winterish coat and my gloves (the steering wheel will be cold). We arrive early and listen to the choir warm up. Very nice. It will be Mozart's Kroenungsmesse (Kroenung = the crowning), she said. The cleric procession arrives and the organ blasts mighty tones into the church. The air is full of smoke scented with myrrh. Yep, I can recognize Mozart when I hear it. Almost everything must be fortissimo. It is giving me the goose bumps. It was St. Peter who came first to the empty grave, so the priest says. I thought research has found out it was Magdalene? But the organ, the choir, and the beautifully cold landscape outside put it right again for me. Thank you for dragging me along. Let's go home and see what my snow covered Magnolia tree is doing.

Notes from the 48th North

Sent: Sunday, 22 April 2012 ~ 5.43am

Oh, hello, Isolde! Haven't seen you in over a week, how come? I was away for a while. What do you mean away? Did you visit your husband? No, I visited a friend. A friend? Who and where was your friend? In France. In France? Did not know you had a friend in France. Where you in Paris? No, I was in Provence, Nice, Cannes, and so. Oh, how nice! We did not know you where gone, but when I saw your cousin open your front door with a key we figured you must not be here. Was Steven with you? No. What no? You went without him? Did he know about it? Albert! Well, you by yourself in France! I would have told him. He did not mind? Albert! Well, don't married couples go together on vacations? Albert – can I have my Brezen, and my milk, and my freedom? Thanks for watching my house, though.

Notes from the 48th North

Sent: Wednesday, 23 May 2012 ~ 8.37am

Finally, the undoing of a ski accident has taken place, three months after it happened. Steven has been successfully operated on his shoulder yesterday afternoon. I saw him then late evening. He looked pretty groggy and pale. Today he still has the nerve block med dripping into the relevant nerve in his shoulder and some other drainage tube is still attached. But his natural color was back, he walked around with me carrying the box that supplies the pain medication. Most importantly, he was back to his usual jokes albeit in moderation. But the best post-op thing that happened to him is that his hospital room window is providing a panorama like view over a construction site. And it is not a small one either as the hospital, apparently, is building a whole new wing. So we stood there by the window and he explained to me what I saw. How can there only be fifteen people on this construction site? Well, if you come home on Friday, you might never know. Do you want to stay longer to find out?

Notes from the 45th North

Sent: Sunday, 17 June 2012 ~ 8.42am

It was a smooth flight so far. I have been staring out the window since we started to cross the Alps in south-easterly direction. The peaks were still covered in snow, looking inviting to ski again. But no, I had enough of cold and winter. I was on my way to warmer climes. My partner was asleep next to me holding his arm in its sling protectively. I let my thoughts wander over the past three weeks and other issues that needed to be closed. Gradually I became aware of a long winding river below. Looked silverish gray, running north, big knee, down south and north-east again, like it could not make up its mind which way to go. I got fascinated by it, by its size and path. Where were we? Must be around Belgrade. This was the Danube! Long, wide, winding, with many small islands in it, elongated, aerodynamic, shaped by the water's flow. It felt good to see the Danube. And my thoughts took up the feeling. It always felt and feels good to see the Danube. Actually, this is my river, part of what means "home" to me. My father had been born at the banks of the Danube where it makes a sharp bend south-eastward. I had been born where the river leaves Germany and Bavaria, crossing into Austria. That river's name has always been an intrinsic part of my family history. It is part of who I am, part of where I came from, part of my identity, and part of me as a sort of archetypal blueprint. And my eyes followed the Danube until it moved over the easterly horizon. I turned back into the cabin looking at Steven. He was awake. A penny for your thoughts? With leaving the Danube I am leaving home. Do you have a river or a body of water that you consider part of your roots and identity, part of your baseline? He thought for a while and I thought I knew his answer. Could only be the Columbia River. Yes, he said, the Pacific.

Notes from the 32nd North

Sent: Thursday, 21 June 2012 ~ 1.58am

This is not only about the land of 1001 tales but also of 1001 questions and answers. And they are open to interpretation – concerned, friendly, loving, kind, polite, suspicious, facetious, good behavior, contact seeking, all of the above. Take your pick or watch for clues. I have decided to use all of the above.

Steven tried to swing his carry-on up into the compartment above his seat. Watch out, he warns the other passengers. Oh, Sir no, let me do that. May I help? Two of them jumped up to complete the task. They did not forget to lift it down after a four hour flight! They really are gentlemen and scholars.

Merhaba, Sir, so nice to see you back. How is your arm? So spoken by the hotel manager and the personnel including the fitness studio guy. The breakfast waiter takes one look: How is your arm, Sir? The lunch waiter, the ... Where did you have this operation done? Why not here in our country? And how do you answer that, Sir? You think you are through now, my love? You have not been in your office yet! Steve, how have you been? How is your shoulder? Can we ski again next winter? Do you have a physic here already? So glad you are back!

I think he loves it!

I am all right. But NOOOO, don't touch my shoulder, please! How are you, Isolde? Is he a good patient? I do my best to answer. Lovely people, with all the pain endured we sure deserve such a warm welcome. It feels good.

I will go to the pool tomorrow. Nobody knows me there. I'll mind my own wind blown, salt air business. Relaxation, dreaming, reflecting, planning on. Thank you. But first I have to earn it. I'll swim twenty laps for my back and my figure. But this lady always is in my lane with her sun hat and without caring about my efforts. Attention, Madame, I warn her. What, why? Just don't want to swim into you as I am on my back mostly and can't see you. All right, she says drifting off. But she drifted back the next day. Where are you from? Germany. I swim faster. And you came to Lebanon? Yes. Why? Husband is here. Oh. Do you like Lebanon? She shouts after me. When I come swimming back she says, do you like Lebanon? Of course. I'll go to the office tomorrow. Cross the parking lot to shorten the way. Hi madam, are you from Gerrrmany? The parking lot attendant asks. How did he guess? Yes. Oh, Gerrrmany football verrry good. You like? Nam, habibi, I shall go swimming tomorrow. But don't I love the attention, though?

Notes from the 32nd North

Sent: Sunday, 8 July 2012 ~ 8.33am

I was once more, like often before, sitting on a terrace high above the shore in Beirut watching a spectacular sunset. It always has a melancholic effect on me, eliciting a certain sadness, undefined, while enjoying the turning of the earth. It was no exception last night. But that night suddenly it came back to my mind what I have regretted before: Where did all the dolphins go?

A long time ago, when looking into the Mediterranean southward from the Riviera coast of Italy I sometimes had the pleasure to see a group of them. Where are they now, what happened to them? And I realized that I have asked the same questions about my lost friends from all the various places before. Where are they? What happened to them and our friendship? How has life been for them? Deidra from California, Mary Beth from Arizona, Viktoria from Bolivia and Washington D.C, Craig from Houston, Barbara from Houston, Mark, Chantall from La Varenne, Rena from Cairo (names changed). I feel the loss of them acutely, time and again. I obviously still have unfinished business in my past. Perhaps *Far Away from the Brewery* indeed needs an extension? It is good to remember those that stayed on even though we are by no means living in any kind of vicinity.

Even Switzerland and Austria seem too distant at times, not to speak of the UAE or New Zealand. But we have an inner closeness that has not changed. And that is the balance to the losses, healing, but not completely. Those losses will always matter to me somehow. Of course, these days I should not watch sunsets maybe. I have another very painful immediate loss to deal with. I lost my wedding ring on my last plane ride, not to be found again. I have had it on my finger just shy of forty years.

Loss is a subject in my life, Isolde's Unfinished Symphony, so to speak. For the time I try to focus on new friends in Beirut. But those I will have to leave at the end of this week as well. Life is a journey. I need to accept that. Many happy returns, as my Indian friends from Dubai always say.

Notes from the 32nd North

Sent: Thursday, 12 July 2012 ~ 6.44am

Tomorrow perhaps a few more laps in one of those salt water pools, but that's it. Then the closing word applies that I once upon a time learned from Umberto: Ultimo Banjo! It was so rejuvenating and invigorating.

But you, my beloved Mediterranean, forgive me for not even setting my big toe into your waters. You have a brown sprinkled appearance. Never did figure out what it consists of. And your carpet of plastic, cups, sheets, bags, rugs and more unspeakable things, that you have swimming along your rocky and sandy shores have turned me off. I am disgusted with you. Of course, you do not have dolphins jumping out of that pollution. Who has corrupted you so? Sometimes the winds have driven the whole mess out to sea, but it always came back in. You, the gentlest of the oceans of this globe, where one cannot even observe the tides changing, with so many songs made for you, with so many stories, love stories as such, with so many poems dedicated to you, how come your dignity has been so disregarded? You used to heal me in mind and body. And against the odds – you still do. I will leave you again, but I will not leave you to your fate. I'll do what I can to help.

And you, my dear Beyroute, you sure are a native Mediterranean. Love your corniche and the fact that you keep the beaches relatively free for everybody to enjoy. But you have a whole lot more potential. Your people I admire for their ability to live with whatever life may have in store, and that without giving up laughter as a coping strategy. Many of your people grow up trilingual as a matter of course. And I take my hat off to you when I can hear church bells ringing and a Muezzin call for prayer almost at the same time. Your people have taken me to the doctor when I was sick, you have invited me, you have driven me around with care. And just yesterday night you did not laugh at me when I thought I heard one thousand frogs quaking. No, you said, these are our crickets. Pray tell me, how big are they that they can make such a racket of noise?

I wish you stability, prosperity, and most of all, peace in your lives. Ma' a salema, I am not abandoning you. Let's keep in touch. I will go up the globe a ways to the 48th North.

Notes from the 48th North

Sent: Sunday, 29 July 2012 ~ 8.28am

You know how to go to Munich Airport? It is easy, really. First, you rise and shine at 5.00am by the sound of your mobile alarm. Then you leave the house at 5.30am. It's the best time as there is wonderfully fresh air to breathe, there is morning dew, there is a mysterious light and a sinking moon. There is little traffic as it is a time before rush hour. Never mind the trucks, any of them, delivery trucks, concrete transporting trucks, bakery trucks, gasoline trucks, moving vans from Rumania, Italy, Belgium, Holland, Germany, France, and other places, flower trucks, car moving trucks, do-not-light-a-fire- dangerous trucks, and such. Piece of cake, really. Then you drive off speedily until you enter the autobahn. There things slow down a little as they have to do repair work during school summer recess. Then you stop behind the break lights of the truck in front of you. Do not strain your neck to make out the reason for this halt as the line goes over the hill on the horizon and you can't see a thing.

As you stand still you orient yourself in space and time. Ask your passenger when he has to be at the airport. We still have time, he will answer that invariably. After that you wait for twenty minutes in standstill mode. Then you ask your passenger when he has to be at the airport at the latest. Well, let me think, he says. Then he pulls out his iPhone, which he flashes in the rising sun, and he calls our time-honored Italian taxi company. I need a cab at the road next to the road construction site on the autobahn near Ampfing. Then he hands the phone to his wife and asks whether she can explain to the taxi driver where he wants to be picked up. What? the taxi driver asks. She explains that he needs to go on the parallel road to the autobahn up the steep hill. Then the passenger kisses his wife, gets out of the car on the autobahn, grabs his suit jacket, puts it on, grabs his briefcase and says: Sorry to leave you here, I have to catch my plane to London. I'll call you. How much money do you have with you? I need the taxi fare please. Wife changes to the driver's seat, moves it forward. Then the departing passenger slams the car door shut and climbs over the barrier.

Then he starts climbing up the steep hill, slides back, tie flapping in the wind. He finally reaches the top through all the long grass, doesn't brush the seeds off his suit, stands there and waits. Wife sits in the car and waits. Suddenly the truck in the back starts his engine. Wife starts engine, slowly drives forward. Passenger looks dumb and undecided. Should he make a run for the departing car? Taxi comes and picks up passenger. Bye, thanks for letting me sit in a traffic jam of which there seems to be no end. Wife turns on car radio Bayern 3. There is a turned over truck since 3.00am and clean up work will take another estimated hour. Wife waits. Trucks start moving again. After another twenty minutes car reaches traffic circle and has to stop right before entering. Passenger calls and asks where wife is now. He tells that that taxi driver wanted to re-enter traffic jam further up the road as this is the road to airport. No! passenger (taxi passenger now) yells. Go left and drive to Heldenstein. But this stretch of road there is closed to all traffic. Don't care, passenger yells.

Everybody else who could get out of that line of trucks on the autobahn is coming this illegal way, does he not see? Taxi driver gives in. Wife waits in traffic jam. She starts a conversation with frustrated truck driver in front. Passenger (taxi passenger now) calls again and asks how far wife has progressed. She is at the circle. All right, you made it then, passenger (taxi passenger now), exclaims happily. Go around circle all the way, he advices, and take the parallel road home. Wife would have done this anyway. She is broke as well. She is going home and takes a Schnapps for breakfast. No, that is not true! Did he get his plane? Yes, of course, no problem!

Next day wife meets one of the taxi drivers of that company at the butcher shop. What was going on yesterday? she asked. You usually call a day before and we pick you up at the farm. What happened? Wife explains. Taxi lady answers: Our driver was tired but happy to go to the airport as he likes to go there but does not get a chance that often as he usually, like yesterday, drives nights. Did your husband get to the airport on time, did he get his plane? Of course, why should he not?

Notes from the 48th North

Sent: Sunday, 12 August 2012 ~ 3.50pm

It's the month of the comet tail crossing Earth's path. This year I am lucky. Our night sky is free of clouds and as sparkling and mystifying as can be. Yesterday night and today I had the pleasure and luck to see meteorites shoot across the sky and burn up – always a most thrilling experience. I tried to imagine that I am actually in the middle of this all, a mind game that I can only win intellectually; no way do I feel it! All the stars and the Milky Way – yep, clearly visible tonight – bring me closer to feeling like the Little Prince. Small, curious, mystified. Small, yes, like the dust particles left behind by the comet, I mean analogue. Problems tend to be smaller as well when I come back from outer space. Earthen things lose importance. Don't worry, by tomorrow morning I'll be back to normal.

There comes my son, bare-chested as he felt hot inside. Temperature is about 16C – summer midnight temp, yes. What are you doing out here, Mama? I am stargazing and waiting for the Meteorite shower. Oh! Now there are two of us talking about our astronomical knowledge (after all he did belong to his school's astronomy club when living in Egypt), standing in the pitch dark outside. You should go to Australia, Perth. Comets don't stay that long, my son. They are travelers, and you know that those have to move on. And there they go! Wow, cool! Absolutely a thrilling experience. We notice that we are shivering though and dash back inside. It was well worth losing a few hours of pre-midnight sleep.

And when have you visited your stellar home last?

Notes from the 48th North

Sent: Friday, 31 August 2012 ~ 2.09am

According to the weather report, this is the last of those very warm, dry, blue sky summer days and a full moon night. That's the time to have an evening and part of a night at our very own miniature Oktoberfest. It is so hot under that huge tent, the music is also hot, and people seem to have fun as judged from their behavior. Then we go to take a look at the hottest rides. This is not the Oktoberfest, have done scarier ones before, so they say and decline. One is even ready to call it quits early. That one the next day reports sensuous overload from too many people, too much noise, too many clashing colors of the Dirndl dresses and too many sweaty breasts. Fair enough, you guys up north are not used to so much fun.

But today you might calm down when the caterpillar rumbler is digging three trenches for the pipes to be laid out to reach their destinations. Now this is really fun, bearable fun. In the evening there is even more fun because the connections are resistant and a thunderstorm is forming in the west. And now the dripple, and now the downpour. Do you see how the trenches fill with water, muddy water, like the Nile used to flood before the Assuan Dam (Aswan Dam) was built. Put on your boots! The pipe needs to be cut? Get me the metal saw, please! No, get me the other saw. Damn it, give me the electric one. There is the fun: standing ankle deep in muddy water, using an electric tool (somebody hold an umbrella over this and give me my raincoat), and get the light from the flashes of lightening from the thunderstorm. Has anybody here ever had physics or biology or meteorology? No? It is well known that it does not take those specialists on a construction site. It takes a psychologist, or any other mental health professional who has been taught effective coping skills, one who can keep calm in the midst of that kind of fun. And one that can, during a late evening dinner, prepare the workers for tomorrow. Because tomorrow at 1.00pm we are going to pour concrete again. Some psychologists are not beyond freaking out, though!

That is the fun of construction sites and the Rubber Boot Dance. Who could disagree?

Notes from the 48th North

Sent: Friday, 21 September 2012 ~ 8.57pm

Mama, when did you say Papa is coming?

He will arrive Wednesday, I mean tomorrow evening, 9.30pm, Turkish Air, Terminal 2. Could you please pick him up at the airport?

Yeah, I will. The hour and fifteen minutes drive back is always good for a nice talk.

Thanks, I'll take him to the airport on Thursday then. Why, Thursday?

He has to go to Geneva.

He is arriving tomorrow evening and leaves the next day? What time? Thursday afternoon. Have to leave the house about 1.00pm. How long is he going to be gone?

Coming back on Friday late afternoon, Lufthansa, Terminal 2. Can you pick him up?

Yeah, I will. But then I have to pack, Mama. I know. You are leaving when exactly?

Plane leaves at 3.00pm. Need to leave the house at about 12.30. Okay, I'll take you to the airport on Saturday then.

Friday afternoon: I have changed my departure, Mama, I'm leaving on Sunday at 3.00pm.

Spotlight on a Stream of Consciousness

You mean nobody has to go to the airport or arrives there on Saturday? Yep!

Gloria Hallelujah, we can sleep in! No deadline! No wheels! Yep, we can. But are you taking me to the airport on Sunday? Of course! We leave at about noon, Air Berlin, Terminal 1? Right!

Monday morning: Darling, can you pick up Bart from the airport? He is coming in at 22.00, Air Berlin, Terminal 1.

I'll do that … together with you, my dear. Let's make a half night at the airport, have dinner at "Airbraeu" there. Their garden is very romantic at night as you know.

Then we pick up Bart and you drive back because night driving is not so much my thing.

Good idea, we both go and have a date at the Munich airport. Haven't done this in a long time!

Thanks, I knew it! Who could pass up a date at the Munich airport?

Notes from the 48th North

Sent: Monday, 8 October 2012 ~ 9.36am

That was it for 2012. Yesterday was the last day of the Oktoberfest. With the goodbye song "Sierra Madre" the flow of beer stopped and an hour later the doors closed. It was a rainy day, that last Sunday. Yes, he said, he wanted to go anyway. Of course, if you are young, from the flatland of Berlin, and never have experienced this madhouse of "Wies'n" than you have to go. And I took him gladly. He entered the first beer tent in his life. At 11.00am we were able to find two seats still. When the music started at 12.00am sharp it lifted him off his seat with the bang it made. He was brave enough to go on the five-looping's-ride after lunch and a liter of beer. And some kind of a trip it was. Soon as he was buckled in the rain started and developed in no time flat into a fierce downpour. The little wagons raced their rounds straight, lopsided, up into every loop making people hanging in their seats upside down. There was no way to close the jacket. He came back grinning and soaked to the skin. Still was a good ride, he said. A bit disoriented at arrival but an experience of a kind and a story to tell back in Berlin. I took him up to the Patrona Bavaria, about thirty-metres high in itself and located up on a hill, watching over the Oktoberfest year after year. My goodness, lots of people, he commented looking down into the place. No, Bart, these are not beginning to be "many" at all. The rain, you know. They are in the beer tents. So back in we went. It was full to the fullest – about 8000 people. He stood and watched silently. Some were already standing on the benches, and some on the tables. And counting – until the song "Sierra Madre" and the security makes them come down and pack up. See you next year if the creeks don't rise. Your new love? Goodbye until next year. Unless of, course, you exchanged mobile numbers. If you have lost yours, go to the lost and found office. Each year they collect thousands of mobiles under the rides. – And they drink six milliliters of beer, they steal 110,00 mass krug, they eat 116 oxen, the Bavarian Red Cross usually treats 8000 patients, 800 of them are alcohol victims. Four million people come by public transport to the one and only station – Theresienwiese. In these two weeks that station was closed 124 times because it was so full that it became dangerous.

You want to come again to get the feel of Oktoberfest on a sunny day? Yes, for this was an experience like no other for me, he said. The downpour over the looping ride was just a special feature. It was a great day! I know they say that being part of it is everything. Okay, but now let's catch the train and go home. We need to dry ourselves out.

Notes from the 48th North

Sent: Sunday, 21 October 2012 ~ 6.41am

They are all gone! It is so quiet around here. I was looking forward to getting my personal space back, my time, my following my own interests undisturbed, continuing writing my story. But now it turns out to be a challenge of readjustment to exactly that. I may be engaged in some activity and suddenly jump because nobody has knocked on the door, called for me, or simply walked in. That rhythm evidently is still in me. No wonder, these have been four intensive weeks of demolition of familiar space and reconstruction. The knocking away with a hammer was knocking away at an era as well. We had four different nationalities in our crew, external and internal. We got along well, understood each other despite a Babylonian problem. We worked, laughed, swore, and took care of each other. One of them I took to mountains, lakes, historical places, and Oktoberfest with great pleasure. As the only female in this crew I was treated with deference. But today, a day of fog and overcast skies with a distinct flair of autumn, romantic, melancholic, and harsh simultaneously is driving home the issue: I am left to my own devices and physical freedom. Just the weather to bring about the corresponding feelings. But what do you expect? Everybody went home to a safe place, except one that flew off to a country and a city in crisis. Just received a phone call after him leaving that airport: Everything quiet on the eastern front. So I was reassured. I'll hang on to this until I hear tonight's news. Meanwhile I'll enjoy a walk in the brisk fall air, the vivid colors of trees getting ready for frost and snow, the birds on the new roof fighting for a warm place for the winter months, the hot spicy apple cider with my schoolmate, the soundless moving of the dense fog creeping up from the valley, Albert happily accepting my gift of walnuts, reading the concert and theater guide of Munich and Salzburg for the season. We shall not all hibernate in winter. "We shall overcome" melancholy. Actually,

I should say – allow it. And I remember fondly the day s, weeks, and often months in Munich when we were teens and met exactly because of weather that tried to get us down. We were together, had fun, roamed around in our city that seemed to turn out its best for the dreariest season. Who cared about weather? Human beings are social animals. Long live that characteristic of ours.

My love to you!

Notes from the 48th North

Sent: Friday, 26 October 2012 ~ 7.07am

Another one of those overcast, dark, dreary, foggy, moist, awfully still, late October day s. The light fog makes the forests and meadows appear like a, well, foggy notion in the distance. Yet, the trees in their brown, yellow, and red crowns sprinkle bright dots of color into the milky background. Life is getting ready for hibernation. To me it looks like a live impressionist scenery, vague, hinting, beautiful, serene, and peaceful. I am standing by the window and think back to another October day, a bit sunnier than this one. I also was getting ready – ready to leave my home for the blue yonder of Australia. I was stepping into a relationship that I have been warned about for a few months prior to that day.

This is mad, I was told, it is too risky. This can never work. What do you know about this man? You have never seen his home. And besides – the US, his home, is such a dangerous place. Good thing you go to Australia instead. But what if he dumps you there? This is an international relationship, they usually work out bad. Why do you do this? Could you not find somebody from us? Nobody good enough for you? Has to be exotic! And than that one: If I just hear this name – Steve! Why somebody from so far away! And then him: She is going where? To Australia? Well, why not to the moon, Isolde? Are you coming back? Only one, my dear friend with whom I have shared so many Saturday evenings in the Munich discos, with whom I have been skiing in the Bavarian Alps, whom I visited in London, and much more, only she allowed for some tears and a positive attitude to my endeavor: *Gute Reise und alles Gute. Ich habe viel von dir gelernt* (happy journey and good luck. You have taught me a few things), she said. She is still my friend, since a long time in an international marriage herself.

Tomorrow, that same Steve and I intend to go to Munich, to the place where we have exchanged our first kiss, forty-one years ago, and intend to do the same again. Then we will visit the Wittelsbach fountain, where we use to meet. Yesterday was our fortieth wedding anniversary and tomorrow, forty-one years ago, we boarded that plane that took us to Sydney, Australia, and to a wonderful whirlwind life together. Now the critics and doubters have been silent for many years. There is another question pertinent instead: How the hell did you do it? I don't know for sure, but I am sure glad I did listen to you all and then follow my own intuition, my gut level feeling, and my heart. I am grateful!

Notes from the 48th North

Sent: Friday, 9 November 2012 ~ 6.29am

Like almost every day, I sat down in front of my morning program on TV with a bowl of cereal and a hot cup of tea. The pale winter sun came through the glass door and let the dust particles dance on its rays. Tranquility! I felt good and ready for the day. There – my attention was captured by a huge and beautiful gush of water shooting into the sky out of the North Sea. What's it about? I was all ears. This, so the journalist explained, was the result of a WWII bomb exploding on the bottom of the sea. Is she serious? We all know that the Baltic Sea is full of dangerous, poisonous, and radioactive crap. But the North Sea? A few bombs left over perhaps? Why not? No, my dear ocean lovers. As we are about to grind electricity producing windmills, by the thousands perhaps, in the ocean bottom and drop the cables necessary to transport that energy and other devices necessary for modern communication, we discover more and more of those things that were pushed and dropped into the North Sea at least sixty-seven years ago. I am still not sure I heard that correctly when she said there are "a few million tons" of deathly stuff down there amongst the famous North Sea herrings and crabs. One bomb or sea mine can contain half a ton of the lovely powder. Another sweeping death device is nerve gas slumbering and eroding away in the North and Baltic Seas. Thousands of tourists and bathers, windsurfers and Wattenmeer lovers run across the sandy, windswept beaches. Kids are jumping around in the flat waters of the surf and dig in the sand. A beautiful, relaxed atmosphere is oblivious to the hidden death potential nearby. The ying and the yang, the beauty and the beast, the good and the bad, healing and destruction, love and hate, and let's hope the past but not the future. So which beach could I go to and enjoy without a care in the world? Happy holidays in the healing powers of nature. Sorry if I spoiled your breakfast.

Notes from the 48th North

Sent: Saturday, 8 January 2012 ~ 5.53pm

It's the time where everything closes down, quiets down, stops. Even construction sites slow down for winter, the snow covered months. It was touch and go for the whole last week. Will we still get the ceilings in, everything dry enough? Yes, we will, we even will pour concrete in both rooms. It ain't freezing yet. We actually make it, even though it is already freezing by the time, two days later, when the second load of concrete is being poured. And then everything is suddenly finished. Six workers are gone. Conrad has left for Berlin.

It is so quiet in the house that I can hear my own nerves sing. I feel myself coming down, feel lost, stranded. (I repeat myself, I know). Won't have any enthusiasm to tend to my story again. What am I going to do with myself? I have a head cold that makes me lethargic, don't feel like applying my healer of Nordic walking across country either. Well, somehow I will get readjusted to single life. I start with going grocery shopping in Albert's store. You are by yourself, again, Isolde? Has Steven left, has Conrad left, have the workers left already? Wow, thank you for asking, Albert. He cares perhaps and thus helps some.

Next healer is my computer, sort of. There is a note from my friend from Vienna: Isolde, I am in Munich. Let's meet. Bless your heart, Gabri. You came just at the right time. I'll be there early next week. That is really good. It's the foggy, snowy, melancholic night settling in by now. My brother calls. Are you by yourself again? Conrad also gone already? What are you doing in the evening? Don't know, brother, have yet to reorient myself. Don't get down, he says, take a hot bath with some eucalyptus stuff in it against your cold. Thanks, I might just do that. The telephone rings again. Hi, Regine, what's up? We are going to a choir concert. Would you like to come with us? Without hesitation I accept the invitation. How did they know already that I am by myself? Those two are always fun to be with, choir concert or not. Thanks for being you!

Notes from the 48th North

Sent: Saturday, 22 December 2012 ~ 5.32am

This is the season to be jolly, the season of love and gifts, and the season to remember the cause that brought on this season in the first place. Love would include the renewal of friendships far and near, long ago, or recent. I often have felt a bit humbled by the friends that remembered me Christmas time when I did not reach out to them. One of my long term and close friends had dug out my only permanent address that I had given her just in case her and my nomadic life style might wipe out our paths. It did, and after three years I got a note from her. We never lost each others tracks again. That is long distance friendship for you. But this year one long term, long distance, many years colleague and friend has humbled me the most.

I am going to be in Germany a few days before Christmas, she mailed. I am going on a tour with my kids. We are flying to Budapest (from California a formidably long distance flight).

From there we are going the Danube upriver and will be in Passau for a day or so. I contacted my husband and read it to him. Do you think she means it as this is quite a tour? You mean she is traveling from California to Hungary? Yes, that's what it sounds like. Well, it does not *sound* like it, this is what it says. Finally it sank in! And I started the you-are-kidding-route for a while. And then I began to calculate: I have seen her last in 2004 at the art therapy conference in San Diego! That makes eight years! I can't believe this. How lucky I am. This is a Christmas gift of another kind. I am coming to Passau, by hook or by crook, snow, sleet, or avalanches. Nothing can stop me! And we did meet.

It was a feeling of utter pleasure when I saw her face change to an expression of recognition and joy. I hugged her tightly and felt the same back. There were eight years in this hug and all the years that we have walked our profession and friendship together far apart or close. We spent but a mere three or four hours together that day of reunion. But that was not the issue at the end. Much more important and telling was the fact that we seemed to pick up where we left off last time eight years ago in San Diego. There was, so to speak, no distance between us. It was one of those happenings in life that I store in my memory to treasure and recall when the need arises.

Merry Christmas to all my fans of my Notes. This is to remember you long or short distance. It is the inner distance, or the absence of it, that does it.

And a happy New Year to you. Should we agree on a resolution? That we won't lose contact with each other.

Notes from the 48th North

Sent: Friday, 4 January 2013 ~ 7.09am

He is taking a bath? That shower fanatic guy? You know why? I mean he is not sick or anything like that, is he? No, not sick, but the days are so dreary, foggy, snowy, dark, you name it. To take a full bath with bath salt in it and stuff, this is luxury. Something like that is what he said anyway. Very well then. The problem is just that he takes so bloody long, like almost two hours. I need to get ready for tonight and need my makeup kit. Well, ask him to come out pronto or ask him to go in and get what you need. You are his mom. So mom was allowed in. She could not believe what she saw! Darling, she came back to her husband, do you know why he is in there so long? No clue – is he fishing? No, he was reading a book! What? He was reading a book? Yeah, would you believe? A book? In the bathtub? What happened? I don't know. Well, this is all weird for he neither has liked baths so far nor did he read books. What is going on? Oh, I guess it is a kindle book, right? That would explain it. No, darling, he was reading a paperback! You mean a book made of paper, not electronic at all? Yes, and not at all! How are we going to respond to that? Well, since it is a first since childhood we should just watch how this develops. It is probably nothing serious.

I am telling you, Anna, he was reading a paperback! Oh, wow, do you know what caused that change? No idea, perhaps he gets a back pain on the computer by now. Or he is afraid to drop the kindle thing into the water! Well, I'll say. No, my son has not done something like that. I would be just as concerned as you are. But then, your Chris, he always has been a bit different than his peers, would you agree? Well, not significantly. Perhaps he has been a bit of a loner sometimes which would point towards the reading of books. Reading books does isolate you a bit from your friends, doesn't it? I agree, but it is not even a kindle but a paperback! Guess he is just not a conformist. Actually he has a streak of defiance in him. Anna, I beg your pardon! Well, sorry, but how would you explain such a switch to reading a tangible paperback where you need to turn the pages yourself, and even in the bathtub! Actually, how does his girlfriend react to this change? Don't know, I am not sure she knows it yet. Oh boy, one o'these days she is going to find out! You are scaring me, Anna, I don't want to listen to you. Maybe he just has matured! Can you say the same of your son? No, but I think you should consult a psychotherapist to make sure he is all right.

Notes from the 48th North

Sent: Sunday, 3 February 2013 ~ 7.44am

Mark Vonnegut, son of author Kurt Vonnegut (*Slaughterhouse Five, Cat's Cradle*), once wrote "Nothing lasts Forever". In light of three deaths of close relatives in our family within fourteen months nothing rings more true than that statement. So we live our life always keeping in mind our temporary existence? I remember our seminars recommending to newcomers any country or place in the world: Don't live like you are camping out in your apartment because you know in two years you will move back home. Think as if you will live there forever. Otherwise you have a good chance of being unhappy, uprooted, with a feeling a having neither arrived or being at home and you may have to welcome depression. So think "forever" for the sake of happiness? Is that a bit paradoxical? Perhaps, but life is diverse, so they say. What is the term then that fits and summarizes such ideas seemingly contradictory? Ambiguity? Yep, both notions have their merits: the transience and the need for stability in life. This is not fair, you are thinking. I am with you. No, it is not. Wasn't there somebody that stated that life is not fair? I admit it was me and my wonderful colleagues. The solution then? Let's live like there is no tomorrow? No, not wild orgies until we drop. Famous people said it: Enjoy the moment (Ghandi and the Dalai Lama). The latter has been asked by a German journalist: When are you ever happy? The Dalai Lama had the answer promptly: Now!

Are you thoroughly confused? Well, that's what I am talking about. Perhaps it helps if you can think at least two dimensionally and tolerate ambiguity. Or are you one of those modern wonders of a multitasker anyway?

Notes from the 48th North

Sent: Monday, 11 February 2013 ~ 9.14am

The world championships in Alpine skiing in Schladming, Austria, are begging me the question how far we can drive competitiveness. I am glued to the TV watching one skier after another go. Wish I had gone there. Look at them tear down the hill. Only speed counts, hundredths of seconds count, every slightest mistake counts. Put your ski too flat? Slows you down. Flying over the big bumps not far enough, three/hundredths of a sec. slower. Could be third or fourth place only. They don't get the straightest line down to the end? They are carried off course by a sheet of ice and miss a flag? Disqualified – after a year of preparation and training, in one fraction of a second it is over. They put spectacular stars into the snow. Actually at speeds from 90–130kmh it is more like the path of a comet until the nets catch them. The first net they might go through, into the second one. By that time the skis are elsewhere on the piste. Helpers come by skiing and running. Can he or she get up? Miraculously, mostly they do. And then they hit the air with a fist, or they jam a ski pole into the snow. Anger reigns, not fear and shock. These are the racers that can't possibly consider injury, only speed and the straightest line to the finish line counts. I am watching with pleasure and occasional horror. I bite my knuckles, by George did you see that? This one was already with her behind in the snow and got back up! How did she do that at that speed? What enormous muscle control! And here goes the world champion from last year. Watch her! Top speed! LindsayVonn. One ski catches! She hits the ground, she is catapulted up again into a salto by outstretched body. Then there is a cloud of snow and the red safety net shoots out into the second safety net. The helicopter lowers the rescue worker down. She is airlifted in a stretcher with two aid people left and right all hanging on a rope. Off to the hospital over the tree tops. There comes the next racer at 110kmh. Don't think about what just happened! You might crash as well if you do, or you lose a tenth of a second time. She makes it okay over the finish line.

Today I watched the men's downhill. The first and the third racer each crashed spectacularly. But they both stood up. The sheet of ice was even bigger today. The show must go on. And I must keep watching. It's a sport that I love and fear. So why am I still skiing? Well, why are they risking their bones, maybe even their life? Have you felt the wind in your hair when you go downhill? I think it is that wind? Or is it the white snow, the blue sky, the sun, the feeling you get on the top of a mountain, that freedom feeling which is, of course, temporary and an illusion anyway? Or the feeling of gliding over snow? It must be the wind!

Notes from the 48th North

Sent: Monday, 4 March 2013 ~ 9.33am

It is a glorious, melancholic view through this window. It's a winter sun still, a cloudless sky, in fact an orange and pink sky. The forest skyline on the horizon and on top of those distant hills is already colored black by the night air and the sinking sun. But the snow covering the land is a wonderful white contrast. I can't hear that evening silence in here in my room but I can see it. I have seen it so often, either when I was still out sledding as a kid, or later when skiing in the Alps, when we came down from the slopes, tired and happy. But this horizon of hills, forests, silence, and orange also sends out the hustle and bustle of the world beyond. There is a vivacious world over that blue and orange yonder. First there would be Munich, then the MUC airport. And I definitely feel the four year itch (it has not been seven years yet) to go to that airport and beyond that horizon. I will, folks, I have been packing my suitcase today for two different climatic zones. I am so looking forward to going and to arriving and finding you all that are still left there. Look out when you see me through your eyes of the desert. I'll be shaking off the Alpine winter (until next year). And did you ever read that promise spoken from, I believe Gaspar, that "morals sink with the sun and both are just nature"? Well, when my plane touches down in the desert of Arabia my morals will not be the issue, but my spirit which will be looking forward to all those hugs of reunion. See you then, inshalla.

And for you, the only one I might not be able to see, please forgive me. I am dancing to the tune of someone else with a tight schedule. I will find a way to make a special time for us, with nothing but spending time together and to visit, revisit and to look forward. Either your place or mine. Wherever.

Notes from the 2nd South

Sent: Tuesday, 19 March 2013 ~ 8.44pm

So please tell me how to say hello in your language? *Bon jour*, he said. No, no, I mean in your own language, how do you say good day and goodbye? *Bon jour* and *au revoir*, he said. I tried it another way. If you meet your friend on the street in Victoria (the capital of the Seychelles) how do you greet him? I probably ask him where he is going. Is he an avoidant personality disorder or is he teasing me? Neither option seemed to be very likely. Tell me, what language do you usually talk in? Well, I am not sure, I think English as we have a lot of English speaking visitors. But we use French as well, and amongst us locals we also talk Creole. Actually, we speak everything, he concluded. I felt I was getting somewhere. So how do you say hello in Creole? Probably *au revoir*, he said with a slight grin but not without sincerity. I began to understand, or so I believed. They have integrated three languages into one, that is, their original language and those two from their colonial masters. A light came on in my head. Have I not done this to some extend myself? I still mix my native Bavarian, German, English, Turkish, and Arabic, add a bit of French and Italian, simply because I have been exposed to those languages growing up in Europe. These people of the Seychelles are my living credo: integrate, and add to your identity throughout life if so challenged. Who are these people then here on these tropical islands? Well, we are Creole, originally, so their answer goes, but we are Seychelles, of course. Of course, who could doubt that?

But they are something else, more than anything. They are laid back tropical islanders. Don't rush, they recommend if not urge you. And I took it to heart expressed with the sluggish, slow way of walking that I have acquired somehow.

In a few days I will cross the equator again in a northerly direction, my eighth crossing. Looks like I might do it a ninth time. And then I'll walk another pace again. Adjust!

Notes from the 48th North

Sent: Thursday, 18 April 2013 ~ 9.49pm

It has been almost three whole days now but certainly three whole nights trying to fit this surprising event into my stirred up mind. The cause, presumably, is my way of letting the past be the past. I do not like to go back, look back yes, for various reasons, but go back – no, not possible. But now I have a little challenge, one that I actually could perhaps embrace. It started out with the innocent ring of my door bell. Since I have a young worker on the farm to bring the neglected garden into shape I did not think anything else but that it was him ringing the bell. Instead there stood a couple, just stood there looking at me. I did not recognize man or woman but I knew instantly that there is something extraordinary about them. Expectant, inquisitive, but also somewhat mischievous eyes looked at me, not to mention the slight grin on the woman's face. And on the woman my attention focused. My brain was searching. After a while there was some dawning taking place. No idea what the length of that *while* was. Yes, it is her. She is a voice and a figure out of my past, the past which had begun in 1971. Before I came around to saying her name she beat me to it: I am Gerlinde, she said her grin having intensified to a lovely, knowing smile. I dropped my arm full of laundry onto the floor. We threw our arms around each other as if we were to make up for the past decades of no contact. It was so wonderful to see each other again, as if we had taken a great detour and came back in one piece, bruised and battered by life, but intact.

As an aftermath to this significant event I am contemplating its impact on me. Certainly my ego feels the nice strokes of having been remembered and sought out and found again. But I am a person who does not look back, can let go of the past. How often did I have to deal with issues that reached from the past out into the present and prevented a given person from happiness in the so called here and now! I do suspect myself though, that I also don't want to be reminded of the blunders and the dumb things I did or said in my past. But I also have become the person that believes firmly in the *who cares* attitude. I am who I am and I became who I am partially because of my past history. So perhaps Gerlinde is offering me an opportunity to pick up where we left off so long ago? I still think this is not possible but I can pick up the moment three days ago and moving forward, gladly adding her and her husband to my here and now circle. Thanks for coming by, you made my day, and you gave me the challenge of rethinking one of my convictions. I like that. I'll see you around.

Notes from the 48th North

Sent: Wednesday, 1 May 2013 ~ 6.20am

I was in a good mood when I went to Albert's store Friday last week. It was early morning and relatively warm, too. The air felt spring-like and light. Isolde, it is time you stop walking around outside with your two sticks all the time, he said with vehemence in his voice and flashing eyes. Well, good morning to you, Albert. Are you okay? Yeah, I just think it is dangerous for you walkers with your sticks to run all over the place out there. As I said, are you okay? Did you not hear the helicopter yesterday at 6.00pm? Don't recall, I might have. But even if I did I don't assign any significance to it. What's up? His eyes grew even rounder and he leaned forward toward me. Anna was run over by one of these liquid cow-shit trucks down there, just where you always walk, too. OMG! How could that happen in the open field and meadow? She had to be flown by rescue helicopter to Traunstein and operated on immediately for four hours, Albert almost shouted. It was his sister-in-law, a dedicated Nordic walker. I know that these trucks are monstrously big and it can run out its "arms" left and right as if it had grown wings the size of a jumbo jet. Somehow she was hit in the back with one of them. The result was disastrous as it broke three of her vertebrae, dislocated a fourth very badly, and, to top it off, caused a concussion. And we all hope that this is the sum total and nothing more is discovered.

I knew I had to walk by there to not let trauma impact take my route away from me. I got goose bumps running over my skin when I reached the place of accident. The grass was still flattened, deep tire marks were in the wheat field. But I could not make out where the helicopter might have landed. I stayed put for a brief while and let my eyes take in the marks of this freaky accident in between a meadow and a wheat field with nothing to obstruct ones view. And then I walked on. I felt I "owned" the place again. She is still in bad condition in the neurological hospital waiting for the swelling to go down. Only then can the real repair work op be done. I hope she will walk there again someday. And if she should be in post traumatic stress I'll offer to walk with her to that place and repeat that until she can walk by it and go on. But most importantly, I count my own blessings. We intend to walk on, Albert!

Notes from the 48th North

Sent: Sunday, 12 May 2013 ~ 7.28am

Good Grief, did you see *Django Unchained*? Started out promising for me – I am in for social critique any time. Then it seemed to me like saturated with satire – I am in it for satire most of the time and where I think it could make a difference. And then it turned bloody. I stood up to close the shutters. Came back, it was worth watching further. And then it turned gory. I said I am going to look out into the night for a little while. Unexpectedly that flick improved, made sense, seemed correct historically, seemed necessary and worth while. And then my son warned me of an upcoming "bad scene". I closed my eyes and ears and still left to return when I figured that nasty scene might be over. Then my husband verbalized my own thought: *This is going on forever!* I left and I came back only to see it turned nasty, violent, bloody, and gory again. I left to brush my teeth and take my make up off to go to bed. And then I came back, and they where riding off into the sunset. Boy these two could shake off multiple traumatic experiences just like that. Anybody else would be in post traumatic stress disorder or the like and need therapy for the next five years. I left to get a shot of Bavarian medicine after stressful encounters and against revolting stomachs: a double pear schnaps. Could not find any. What kind of household is this? Could somebody put his arms around me please?

Notes from the 48th North

Sent: Monday, 20 May 2013 ~ 9.45am

The Bridges of Madison County, don't remember where I saw it the first time. Was a few years ago. I loved it then, although I think I saw a shortened version at that time. But I do remember it was in English. Today I watched it in German. As a result, a few times I thought that some dialogue has changed until I realized that I am listening to a translation. Liked it better in the original. But speaking of "like". For me this is one of the best love stories that I know. Of course, I can relate a lot, i.e. leaving loved people and moving on. And, by golly, I have been in and on the Great Planes, driving to Witchita, Kansas, to Butler, Oklahoma, coming down the Rockies into the flat part of Colorado, driving on for hours, if not days on end with nothing but prairie (or what used to be such) and grain elevators sticking up out of the endless flat planes, driving from New Mexico through the west Texas plains and so on. You are engulfed by serenity, tranquility, cotton fields, corn fields larger than Bavaria, and a feeling of being the only human being on earth, shall we call it lonesomeness? But the love story in *The Bridges of Madison County* is so real, intense, and tragic. And to think that no other than Clint Eastwood starred (and Meryl Streep) and directed such a tender story. There is not one single four letter word in it, no fists, no guns, and no blood, just a love story about two adults. Is there a message in this story? Well, yes, more than one if you like. At the end the mother decides to tell her children about her love affair, or, about the love of her life with the effect that they go to their respective partners in a changed attitude.

You want to watch it? I recommend it as I think it is a wonderful peace of cinema art from the alter ego of Clint Eastwood.

Notes from the 48th North

Sent: Saturday 25 May 2013 ~ 11.20am

Well, folks, let the game begin. For days now the TV stations had a countdown clock on the upper right hand corner featuring the logo of Bayern Muenchen on the left and Borussia Dortmund on the right. It is forty more minutes to go now. All cool pretend has left me and I am in the soccer and Saturday night fever. I am trying to get my cool back by using the line: It's just a game for goodness sakes. Yeah, right, but there is a lot more to it. No matter though. Brother called five minutes ago: Just want to know what you are watching on TV tonight, he says. Guess, my dear bro, he laughs. Is anybody watching it with you? he asks. Maybe my boyfriend. What? No, I'll watch solo. Ah, that is with a bottle of Spanish red wine. The whole area of the Octoberfest Wies'n is filling up for public viewing, in that rain, he says. Well, and the Bayern Stadium is also open for public viewing. They expect 40,000 viewers. So let's go now. Call me when it gets hairy. Yep, shall do maybe, and if the creeks don't rise and they don't have additional thirty minutes to play. And by golly, let's not have a penalty shoot out. Keep your cool, brother, it is just a game. Or so we pretend.

Notes from the 48th North

Sent: Friday, 21 June 2013 ~ 6.53am

For decades now, I have had a knack for case histories, as some call them, or for personal life stories. That's where personality and identity, and self image is evolving on, that's, in other words, what shapes us throughout life. About four days ago the death of Ottmar Walter was announced throughout the media. He was 89-years old. So let me tell you about his life's story as far as I know it and if I may. For, you see, his life is perhaps a tragic example of the ups and downs and his ship coming into the harbor peacefully after all, as far as I know, of course. I asked a twenty three year old soccer player about Ottmar Walter. He had never heard of him, he said. Who is he? Why would I want to know him? Well, he was a soccer player back at a time when there were only amateur players. Nobody became rich from soccer. It was the love for a sport that stimulated the efforts. But first Ottmar Walter was put to the test by rulers that pursued their own agendas regardless. By that time he and his older brother Fritz had been already recognized as enthusiastic and talented kickers of a gray -brown leather ball. But then he had to stop dead in his track as he was called into the Marine-service for a horrific war. He was born inland and not made for the sea. But that was not an issue. As a Marine soldier he survived ordeals that I only can imagine from the verbal accounts of men that also came back from WWII, maimed in body and soul. Ottmar was wounded. In those days that was often considered luck as he was called back from the ditches that meant death almost for sure. After that he became a POW anyway. Once he was released from prisoner of war camp he returned home to his native Pfalz and his soccer team of Kaiserslautern, a wine growing region on the left bank of the Rhine river, a place generally understood as being populated by cheerful people. He healed. His brother Fritz was there. Soccer was perhaps the sublimation that he needed. After

Spotlight on a Stream of Consciousness

fitness had returned he picked up training and serious play together with his brother again. Eventually, he was called into the newly formed national soccer team of West Germany. Although, so the legend says, Ottmar was always seen as the little brother of Fritz, the captain of the first post WWII German soccer team. Nine years after the end of WWII the FIFA had scheduled the second world soccer championship in Bern, Switzerland. It was not at all sure that Germany, West Germany that was, would be allowed in. At the end they could join. After having lost to the Hungarians 3:8 (!) they still made it to the final. What a surprise. And they had to play, for the championship, you guessed it, against Hungary. You also guess what the odds were to win. But if you are a friend of statistics and number games, you also know that the German team still had a chance to beat Hungary. And they did, 3:2. Perhaps you want to read the reactions of the world, not only the soccer world, to that German soccer victory. It was called and still is called *The Miracle of Bern*. So there was Ottmar, one of the heroes of Bern (not my term), after he had faced death daily for years, has been injured and suffered through POW prison. The euphoria lasted for years for these eleven men, most of all for his brother Fritz, the captain. But life went on, new soccer champions came up and it got very quiet around Ottmar Walter and his ten buddies. Until Ottmar made a suicide attempt for reasons not greatly publicized. And then, this went the way things go with the human mind. He hung on until about four days ago when his passing was publicized all over the soccer world and beyond. Condolences and flowers piled up from those who remembered him and the *Miracle of Bern*. That, after all, is for what he is remembered, one of the eleven heroes of the 1954 world soccer championship and member of a team that was barely allowed to participate so shortly after the war. He and his team mates simply loved soccer and wanted to play it. Nothing else. So was he a hero because he was instrumental in beating the favored team of Hungary? Or was it because he and his team mates played against the greater odds of not being wanted there? Was it the immense love for a sport that could heal his soul? Perhaps they play soccer in heaven.

Notes from the 48th North

Sent: Thursday, 27 June 2013 ~ 3.02pm

To go for Nordic Walking or not to go, that was my question. I fought my Id who tried hard to get me to stay out of the rain and wind. But my Superego reminded me to do it for my bones, my heart, my soul, and my figure. And my Ego cautioned to dress against the wet, cold, and storm, reminding me not to do what could make me sick. Well, over the course of these torrential and relentless rains I hope I satisfied all three. I worked in the garden, briefly, of course, I went on my bike and my rowing machines, and I had a yoga session. For the latter two it took both Beethoven's 7th and 'Fireworks' by Tchaikovsky to get me going. But today I went out in my car to go downtown. The first route I took, trying to be smart in terms of avoiding the flooded areas, was closed due to flooding. Turned around and went the unscenic, old, trodden road, and it was open all the way to downtown. And boy, was it ever scenic! Huge glistening lakes had formed in the flat valley between the Inn and Isen rivers. The Scottish cows stayed carefully on a bit of high ground. The airport (gliders and sports planes) was completely flooded. The rivers spilled over their banks and thus looked wildly romantic in their devastating state of high water. When I come home, so I thought, I have to look at our pond and its flood level. I fell in love with it over again. It was completely green with its coat of water cress. So there was no difference in color between it and the surrounding meadow. It looked like the bushes had grown out of the pond. Actually, the pond and the other flooded areas that I had seen looked beautiful and idyllic. I was aware of the destruction the flooded rivers and creeks caused, especially in my city of birth, Passau at the Danube. The Danube, the majestic river, taking in the Inn and the Ilz, two more rivers, joining it at Passau, was yesterday at a level of twelve metres and counting. Half of the city was flooded. But here in the open country the floods looked beautiful, admirable in their power.

But our little pond, well, was just loveable in its quiet, flooded over its banks beauty. I was standing at the window watching a cat coming across the barn yard carefully picking her way around water, shaking her white paws before almost each step. She might just walk into the pond thinking it is a meadow. I had dropped some boards into it for every creature misjudging the appearance of the pond, as a rescue plateau. Disaster and beauty, yes, they can go together, like it or not.

Notes from the 48th North

Sent: Monday, 1 July 2013 ~ 5.46am

A five hour stop over in Munich? At that airport hotel we have stayed once before? Good choice! This hotel is a five star and well deserving of it as it is really an oasis of peace and relaxation from the noise and hustle that defines a busy airport. The thought jumped into my mind as soon as you told me. It's not been quiet since then. You once called me a five star women – also stuck to me since then. But did you forget about the wicked character trait I have? I am wicked – at times, that is, when it comes to you. And now is such a time. I am thinking about a two and a half hour round trip – night time – to that five star hotel to meet a five star man and spend a five hour night with him. No matter that you are my husband – you are still raising those wicked thoughts in me to behave wickedly – never mind our definition of that term between the two of us. It's an opportunity I should not miss – a date with you with a notion of sinfulness to it. And I would walk you to the check in at 5.00am and wish you good luck for those negotiations in Paris. I would be back at the airport to pick you up and take you home in the evening. If I did not have that night vision problem when driving a car over nightly country roads I would implement all of the above. Think of it – a five star man in a five star hotel with a five star women for almost five hours. Yes, you are the one that raises those wicked thoughts in me!

Notes from the 48th North

Sent: Wednesday, 3 July 2013 ~ 9.30pm

Tomorrow is Independence Day. Do you want to have a traditional hoopla – BBQ, hamburgers, spare ribs, corn on the cobs, marshmallows and so forth.? No, not really, he says. Nothing? No, no, something, I have to go to see the doctor tomorrow. Ah, well then maybe we can celebrate that afterwards? No, but I tell you what we can do: Let's go to a beer garden. You mean to a beer garden to celebrate the 4th of July or your doctor's visit? Neither, just have a German-American evening. Okay, should it be warm enough a summer day that we actually can sit in a beer garden without freezing, yeah, we actually could just celebrate that summer day then?

Okay, he say s, won't spy on your Facebook either. Don't worry you are the only US guy, good looking guy that is, that I would want to spy into my Facebook account. He laughs. The other spying we are thinking about is not suitable for friends. You don't spy on friends (or on your wife), or, else you drop the term "friend". Do they know that a broken trust cannot really be reestablished again? Perhaps we could discuss the issue of broken trust over my Weissbier and your Pils? Who actually is driving the car home? Okay, make that alcohol free Weissbier for me. Let's go and celebrate that Bavarian summer day. There have not been too many so far this season. Happy 4th of July, my dear. Lift your Masskrug – prost to our international union.

And, a posit twice over to you, my dear friend down in NZ. Happy Birthday to you. You are the best reason to celebrate the 4th of July. A big hug and a kiss to you!

Notes from the 48th North

Sent: Thursday, 18 July 2013 ~ 3.29am

Yes, it is true. I have to admit that I did not try hard to re-integrate. Did not really want a place on the totem pole hierarchy of my childhood home. Still can't see a place, or rather my place. Was almost afraid to fit in as I have a different identity, an identity I identify with. Yes, I mean that. I mean I like it this way, I am in peace with it. But to re-adjust back, no. That is not me, otherwise I would be a fake. But I also have not actively resisted. I went, and I am going to the happenings here that I enjoy. And actually there are plenty. So there is a balance that has established itself almost without my doing. Perhaps I am even more re-integrated than I realize. For she floored me yesterday. She saw me tending the garden. Isolde, wait, how are you this morning? Good morning, Hella, how are you? You have a minute? I need to talk to you. Isolde, we are in the process of forming an exercise group, once a week. I am supposed to ask whether you would be willing to run it. Run it, what do you have in mind? Well, would you be the leader and coach? Yep, I was dumb founded, staring into her face and comprehending not too swiftly what she just had said. Gradually I got the imp act. Hella, I am not a physiotherapist, I am psychotherapist. I am not qualified or permitted to work as a coach. Yes, we know that, Hella said. But we (always the "we") know that you have done a lot of sports and fitness for yourself. And we see you exercising. After more of weighing the odds back and forth I agreed that I'll do to them what has been done to me by physiotherapists since I turned eighteen. If they cannot find somebody else that is. Hella smiled when she left and said that she will get "back to me."

But me, I am left standing and thinking about the implication of this request. I admit that it pleased me, made me feel good. But pray tell me, do I have a higher up place on the local totem pole than I knew? The annual dinner of the hunters union suddenly surfaced in my brain. I saw myself entertaining the diners (and the chief hunter of this district who is a friend of sorts of mine come to think of it). Were there processes going on despite myself? Have I actually passed the re-entry phase of an expat repatriating? Did I miss something because arrogantly I thought I already knew that I won't be able to "go home again (Thomas Wolfe)"?

Still feels like – no. Perhaps I should write another book to become clearer in my mind: "Return to the Brewery".

Notes from the 48th North

Sent: Tuesday, 8 August 2013 ~ 1.39

Catch a falling star, put it in your pocket, save it for a rainy day ...

So the song goes. I was out there trying – again. It is the time of year when that particular meteor shower occurs. This time I was lucky to have a clear sky, sparkling with stars. Seldom have I seen our Milky Way so clearly. The Big Dipper was low in the sky. This was the perfect night sky to see every meteor shooting across the heavenly dome. It was so still outside that I could hear the humming of cars on the autobahn three km away. I could see and hear the air traffic over my head as well. The red blinking lights of incoming planes to Munich airport fooled me only for seconds. I turned around my own axis repeatedly to not miss such a falling star. But somehow I must have missed them all. Zip, zero – nothing! Why, why not, it is not possible that there is not even one. I had my wishes lined up that I was going to ask to be fulfilled when a meteorite was flaming in the sky. So here I am with my wish list. I would have needed a meteor shower. Now I have to wait till tomorrow – last day of the heavenly spectacle that has eluded me a few years in a row now. My hopes are up and I am going to try again, if not tomorrow than next August. One item on my list was asking for emails, phone calls, and skypes from my friends. Just for a rainy day.

Notes from the 48th North

Sent: Sunday, 18 August 2013 ~ 7.11pm

She fell in love with the Bavarian forest. Let's take the old road through, Sheila said, not the paved one which makes us mind the cars rushing by (it's my winter picture road). I agreed as it was one of our last walks through such spirit soothing terrain. Her departure time was nearing – five more day s. And tomorrow was reserved for another visit to Munich. It was not a fast Nordic Walking with her, more the leisurely, meandering type. Only farmers with their trucks use that dirt road now. And traffic evading walkers like us two. It was quite overgrown with grass and weeds. That was my undoing. I could not see, and carelessly enough did not expect the deep tracks left and right. My ankle gave way as I stepped onto the high edge of one. It not only pulled my foot out from underneath me but also catapulted me a few steps forward until I hit the ground. It hurt a lot. Stay down, don't get up, stay down, please, Isolde. She was alarmed. She offered to get the car to haul me home. I resisted. Can't be so bad. I can walk back. No, stay down until you are ready to get up! She had suddenly turned into a bossy being. Finally I heaved myself up, made a few steps. Oh boy, the long walk home! I limped forward. Do you want to hold on to me, she asked. No thank you, I answered, thinking: not you with your joint problems. As I walked it seemed to get better and better, well up to a degree. At home Sheila stayed bossy, bossy like a nurse. She put ice packs on my ankle.

I smeared "Gel for Sport Injuries" on. She wrapped it up. And I was mad.

Can't walk through Munich now, probably can't push the gas pedal of my car either. Stay down! Sheila yelled again at home. She cooked a meal, fed me with pie and ice cream, watered the garden – took over. I was grateful – and mad still. Where are your crutches she asked. My crutches? You mean the green ones I had when I had broken my upper femur in 1996? I did not tell her. Half an hour later I saw them leaning against the living room wall. She got them anyway. I was grateful – and mad. I called my husband who I knew was an experienced ankle sprainer.

He was located in a nice lounge chair overlooking the Mediterranean. He had good advice and applied his listening skills. Well, at least now I know what I saved those crutches for all these years. Now as for the swelling ...

Notes from the 48th North

Sent: Friday, 23 August 2013 ~ 9.08pm

This morning my sister-in-law was still sitting at my computer checking out what might be going on at her home in California. Now she is sitting in a plane heading for the Pacific Coast. We had a wonderful five weeks together, cruising through the Bavarian countryside and the Tirolyan Alps, attending medieval festivals and visiting history and natural beauties such as the Zugspitze (2963 m). We spent a crazy day together in Munich walking our feet until they swelled up. Later she was brave enough to go downtown Munich all by herself. She attempted to learn a few German words. Donkey, she said repeatedly which prompted the question "sorry?" with some. No, darling, this sounds like donkey. Say: *daaaanke* – stretch the *a* horizontally. Thank you. But the term that made her exercise for days and cracked up people laughing when they finally recognized the word: *Umleitung*. No wonder, we drove many a detour. Bavaria seems to repair everything during school recess in the summer. Each site told us to drive a detour – a *Umleitung*. But two words she still needs to master: *Auf Wiedersehen!* See you again!

Notes from the 48th North

Sent: Monday, 26 September 2013 ~ 12.15am

My brother and my sister-in-law were here for a Sunday visit. By way of leaving my brother almost demanded that I come for a lunch to their home in Munich the following day as I had to go there for a doctor's appointment anyway.

I agreed gladly. And after lunch I'll take you to Veit Street where you can take the tram into the city. Because, he emphasized, with the tram you can see the city. With you taking the underground all the time you see nothing but a dark hole and an underground station from time to time. Actually, how long ago was it that you took the tram through Munich? He knew the answer and grinned at me like he got me. And he really did that. I hate to tell you. It has been a few decades for sure. So it was that I boarded my old tram number 19 at the street where it turned back going west bound into the city again. This was going to be a nostalgic trip through the part of town that I once lived in. I had fond memories. Remembered my clique of friends, the place where we hung out on weekends, where we played Volley ball, where we went swimming in summer, where we went our different ways to school to get degrees that would lead to a profession which would provide for a life in relative comfort. We were all so bloody young, careless, thinking that the world was just waiting for us. And we then separated for different reasons: a new school, a first job, a first love, first trips out of there to discover the globe. I was the one who went the furthest and never came back: Sydney, Australia. And now I was back! I did not recognize the area. So many more stores, so many no longer existing. The school was gone, the bakery I recognized a few stations after I had passed it.

The whole thing did not match my memory. I had nothing to do with this area. Despite all the modernization, the increased volume of hustle and bustle, the density, the small scale. I shuddered to think that I should have to live here again. I sensed a small scale mind set behind the facade. I felt no familiarity whatsoever and certainly not any of the bliss to be where I once lived a fairly happy life. Quite to the contrary! When the tram finally turned the corner into the East train station of Munich my feelings relaxed and recognition came on that this was my city. That feeling got stronger with every metre. Now that was my city that I feel at home in. It was and is always part of me.

I have yet to figure out what caused that extreme discomfort and rejection on my part of my former home of eleven years. I certainly did not feel any identification with that part of Munich whereas I do with the larger downtown area. This must have something to do with me and the person I became after I left way back in 1971. Having just written this a thought comes to my mind that may give me another clue. We have bought a new car last May and we gave it a license number that includes 1971.

Yep, I think that was where I started to turn my own personal corners.

Notes from the 48th North

Sent: Thursday, 24 October 2013 ~ 5.37am

Already on the train I knew this was the right day to go downtown. The fog was laying low over the land, in the valleys, along the river, and just barely over the little patches of forests. The tips of the tallest trees stood out over the white-gray mass of moisture. The villages along the way showed their church towers reaching into a blue sky. I left the train at the East train station to meet my brother and to cross the Isar river to see its fall appearance with a bit of fog over the waters and the colorful trees lining its banks. We reached Marienplatz, the square in front of city hall, shortly before 11.00am. That's the time when the famous tourist attraction Glockenspiel does its thing, playing the clim-bim music and dancing carved historical figures high up in the city hall tower. How come there are so few observers here today? Where did the crowds go that I usually avoid here? My brother looked at me astounded. Well, the Octoberfest is over, he said. The tourists are gone. Right! We got our city back the way we know it. It was the perfect day to show its true colors. Actually, this was more a summer day in meteorological appearance then fall. The restaurants and cafes had moved their tables and chairs outdoors again. So we also joined the sun seeking population and had lunch outdoors under Chestnut and Ahorn trees with their large leaves now yellow and red. We had a lively conversation about the cars we just had looked at intensively in the Mercedes store at Odeons square. Had never seen the famous Silberpfeil and its contemporary brother of todays Formula One racer so close. The historical Silberpfeil looked more like a rocket in shape. The nowadays car looked like a science fiction thing with every device attached that would make it faster. We talked probably rather animated in our excitement until the soothing fall atmosphere of a calmed down city reminded us ever so gently what a gift of nature this day was. A leaf from the tree canopy above us floated into my plate. My brother laughed. This is dessert, he said. Right, brother. Look into your beer mug. A large yellow leaf looked out over the rim. And since there was a light breeze now more came down on our table. This is nothing, my brother said with a twinkle in his blue eyes. The other day, so he told me, he was under a horse chestnut tree and one of those dark reddish brown fruits dropped into his glass splattering the content onto his t-shirt. We left laughing. That was my city getting ready for winter.

Notes from the 48th North

Sent: Sunday, 27 October 2013 ~ 4.30pm

So we did it again – same procedure as every year. Set the clocks, not the time to be sure, back one hour to winter time for whatever it might be worth. That's fine! I could manage most of my clocks at three in the morning. When I was finished it was 2.00am. But my sports wrist watch wanted to change the date as well. I decided to ignore it until next Spring. Likewise will I proceed with my computerized clock in my car (although I'm sure my son will figure it out by reading a manual written by somebody with a learning disability). The city of Munich employs the Physikalisch-Technische Assoc. (sorry, Les) to change all public clocks, 181 in all, 119 church tower clocks, three clocks of other, historical towers, thirty-nine school clocks, and so fourth (source Suedd. Zeitung, 26.10.2013). How about the time set on computerized, extremely detailed heating systems? You simply have the heating kick in an hour earlier. And then there are the cuckoo clocks by the hundreds or more in the stores and at home. Pray tell me, how do you get the cuckoo to retreat from one too many cuckoo-cuckoos? Friends told me that they can change the time but can't make the bird obey. You just wait until next spring.

Notes from the 48th North

Sent: Monday, 27 November 2013 ~ 11.40am

Yesterday night I had the pleasure to see the movie *Die verbotene Frau* (*The forbidden Woman*). It deals with the love between a woman from the west, speak Europe, and the son of an Emir of an undisclosed Emirate. A true story! Apparently it was the love of a lifetime for both that could not be. The son thought he could pull it through. But the social pressures from family and culture were great and relentless.

Finally, the woman met his bride since childhood, his mother, his sister and she succumbed.

That's the story. Very well. But the film was entirely made in Dubai.

Almost everything I saw was familiar to me in addition to the subject of the film. Consequently, my four years of life in Dubai and those four years in Egypt stood up in my mind very vividly. After the end of the movie my own film kept rolling off in my head. And suddenly the missing light about my foreign life came on. In my book I had made an effort to touch, describe, and explain the feelings about belonging and identity in as an expatriate in a foreign culture and amongst foreign mores I had to come to terms with. I thought I had been thorough. And yet there always was a small corner that I could not get to, until yesterday after I had watched that film. Was that my true feeling of belonging in such different places as the two mentioned? There was the question, always. I felt I had the validity but not the reliability perhaps? Yes, the light came on and blinked the missing link in my brain: authenticity! Where my feelings true but missing a small, last bit of authenticity to be completely true? Now I think so! Why else would I feel a strange ambivalence here in the place of my origins – Bavaria.

Often, since June 2009 I have been struggling with this confusion – a feeling of belonging and yet of foreignness. Authenticity – that is the question. Very well, case solved and hopefully closed as I am very experienced in tolerating ambivalence.

The woman of the above story, btw, now lives happily (so it was written) in Switzerland and has maintained a friendship of sorts with that love of hers.

Notes from the 48th North

Sent: Thursday, 19 December 2013 ~ 2.34am

To my great surprise an email popped up from my Viennese friend. I am in Munich, she informed me. Can we meet? I had not heard from her, as often before, for the better part of a year. Normally she does not write emails. She does not like to look at computer screens at all. Her eyes have set her limits. And she has always had a tendency to "disappear" for a while to resurface again in my vicinity unexpectedly. You see, she has a degenerative eye disease which gives her visual black outs and lets the letters swim pretty soon. She was told that this condition is incurable and it will progress. We hope that it will take a very long time to decline. I was rebellious when she first told me last Christmas.

I refused to believe the prognosis. I have offered her to fly to the US and find some medical wonder that can stop the downward spiral. No, no, no, she said. It is what it is.

You bet we can meet. Tuesday, my dear, at 11.00am downtown Munich. We met where we usually meet, in the reading area of the biggest book store in Munich. Literature has always been a vivacious issue between us. There she sat reading in a book. She dropped it, closed, onto the bench next to her when she became aware of me looking at her. For I took in that she was reading – with her very own eyes. I hugged her as if I could hug the nasty disease out of her. Then I sat opposite her, looking into her sparkling, lively gray green eyes, listening to her exited voice. She was full of life. You would never guess talking to her, spending a day with her, the load she is carrying on her mental shoulders. I admire her for that. Ignore "it" is the motto, move on, and cross the bridges when they come.

Later we meandered a bit through the city, some stores, through the

Christkindlmarkt (Christmas market) with sarcastic remarks here and there, laughing on as if we were seventeen again. She walked with me to my underground station. I hugged her again goodbye and felt a firm hug back. Let me know when you need me. I'll come to Vienna. Me, and your Viennese friends, we won't let you fall. Twenty years of friendship over time and distance (mostly it was a lot further than just neighboring Vienna) have gone passed us. That is a bond, my dear.

And to you, my friends, a lot further distant than Austria, I want to thank you for all the years of long distance and electronic friendship. It ain't easy, I know. But stay in touch. You are so valuable to me and I hope I do the same for you. Because friendship – what is it? It is a form of love, isn't it? It is a place to share, good or bad, a place to be caught when you fall. A place to share life, a place to not be alone, a place to belong. So let me send you an electronic, mental hug, a hug for being there and a hug for your patience to listen to me. Be well.

Merry Christmas and a healthy, peaceful 2014. My door will be open.

Notes from the 48th North

Sent: Saturday, 11 January 2014 ~ 1.46pm

Dear Algebra,

Please stop asking to find your X. She's never coming back. And don't ask Y.

Notes from the 48th North

Sent: Sunday, 9 February 2014 ~ 7.16pm

Having lived an unstable life for so long I still expect this condition in my life. So when signs of steadiness pop up around me I notice and let it reassure my soul that there is an antithesis to the thesis.

The other day I walked over to the village grocery store to pick up a few odds and ends. Inside the door Albert grabbed me by my arms telling me that he needs to ... scold me? I helped him finish his sentence. No, he said, let's call it reprimanding. Careful, Albert! He took a deep breath, still holding me steady. Isolde, listen. Albert, not so dramatic! I am not dramatic, but this is important. It would be good if you would tell Elfi and me always where you are. Are you serious, Albert? I have the feeling you always know where I am. The whole last week we did not see you, not in our store and not out and around anywhere. We did not see any light in your house. Okay, sometimes there was a light briefly. We can't see your living room light because your entrance is blocking our view. Come, he said, taking me to the room with the paper ware and other stuff. Look, we only can see the entrance light and your stairwell light. So when Steven is not here and in his office we don't know what is with you! He looked at me intensely. That way we don't know whether you are home, in the country, or abroad. We don't know whether you are okay over there (over the fence) or sick and in need of help. Elfi joined Albert substantiating his claim. Gradually it sank in that they both are worried when they don't know about my whereabouts. I used the most meaningful term wow to convey my feelings about this. Our two houses have always looked out for each other without ever having spoken about it or made an agreement to that end. It just always was. I have known Albert since he was seven years old. We went to grade school together and played incessantly badminton on the gravel square in front of our house. Likewise the two of us have always supported each other as kids, especially when he cut off one of his fingertips and when his father died suddenly. However, after having lived a life elsewhere and mostly far away and without a connection between us, I certainly did not think I would come back to what I once had left. It flabbergasted me that what once was for childhood friends a matter of course was still there. Sometimes I do find things that stay the same. And for that I am grateful.

How is that for neighbors, Albert and Elfi, folks?

I promised to let them know about my absences and my destinations outside of this village should they be longer or unusual. And here, please keep the key to our house should I lose it once or lock myself out.

Perhaps two years back Albert asked me to play a game of badminton again to see whether we still have it in us. So far it has not happened as Albert had a stroke and was left with a light limp. I think that bugger still needs to win!

Notes from the 48th North

Sent: Thursday, 13 March 2014 ~ 3.29am

As a kid I liked to climb trees, played soccer and later volleyball. I rode a bike, I tried tennis, I walked up the Alps. I ski, I swim, I walk, I do yoga and Pilates. I have always been in sports and I still am. I love the movement and the exhaustion afterwards. I became a real champion in none of them. Later I have often, and I still do, regretted that I was not more ambitious and competitive. It was for me, for the fun, and with friends. But there are days and incidents when I know I should do away with regrets by putting things in perspective. That was done once more for me yesterday when I watched the last Alpine ski events for the season.

She is a double gold medal winner from this year's Winter Olympics in skiing disciplines and a double gold medal winner from the Vancouver Winter Olympics. This, so it was reported, was to be her last downhill race as she considered quitting competitive sports at the ripe age of twenty eight. And she had a very good, almost sure chance to win the combination world championship of this season because her first run was already so good. The day before this race she still had a fever with a bad cold. She had to forgo training. Yet, she stood in preparation for her run up at the start line and coughing. What a determination and how tough can one be? What a need and drive to win! Would I be that same way though? *I hope she is making it okay* went through my head. And there she pushed off and went out of sight in seconds as if nothing was the matter. It looked real good. Then came a left swing about a third downhill the piste. The skis went out underneath her. She catapulted, hit the piste, skidded sideways into the safety net twirling on her back at least three times. The cameras focused on the scene for a while as the helpers came racing to her. It took too long to cut her out of the net. The next skier got the green light to go and filled the screen.

Then the race had to be stopped again in order to let the rescue helicopter come in and hover above the accident place. After a while the helicopter went higher stretching the long rope to airlift. On it hung a paramedic and facing him across his lap was the skier in a collapsed body form. Her back was rounded and the paramedic held her firmly. I still see the picture both of them floating across the mountain, high up to be airlifted to the next hospital. That, as it turned out, was the end of an otherwise glorious, extremely successful skiing career.

In American English I heard that often said: No pain, no gain. No, thank you, I don't regret. There is lots of room for injury in day to day life all by itself.

Notes from the 48th North

Sent: Fri, 21-Mar-2014 5.53pm

Seems like this was the day, yesterday, to return home a little more.

Once again an exercise in memory and identity confused. But don't get me wrong, it was a nice, fond, forgiving, and rearranging-my-head thing. It started at my doctor's office in Munich. Her practice itself is located in a part of downtown where I was often for various reasons. But her nurse put the dot on the I of that beautiful, warm, spring-like day.

Weren't you once in Egypt or somewhere dangerous? Dangerous? Life is dangerous. I was in Cairo, but meanwhile I spent nearly four years in Dubai. Is it dangerous there? Don't know, don't think so, am not there anymore. Where are you now? I am home, here. What? You? And your husband? How is it being back anyway? She was supposed to draw blood and messed up the first attempt. Can I tell you after you have finished sucking it out of me? She laughed. I told her about the toss-up between being happy to have come home and feeling out of place with a strong desire to leave for somewhere.

Her eyes told me that she could not relate but showed a professional "understanding". However, the subject stuck especially tight in my head. Steven and I had just been crisscrossing downtown to get passport pictures taken for a visa. It had to be done by a photographer as the day before the dermatologist had been removing two things from his face. Consequently, his face was neatly plastered with bandages. They had to be "re-touched" from those pictures lest they don't accept them. And where then is the consulate?

It is in Laim, we need to take the S-train. Thank you for knowing things he said. Yep, I did feel good about where to go in this city, my city where I came about.

As soon as we left the underground in that part of town, west of the main train station, I had memory crushing into my mind. That's where three of my friends lived when we all were unmarried or divorced already, respectively. We shared so many good and also not so good times together. We went Saturday night fever dancing, we went to movies we left in the middle, we went to beer gardens, swimming, into the Alps, horse races, skiing, to Judo championships and a few more. Was this the street, let's call him Bert, where we walked across icy sidewalks to a party? And over there we drank Schnapps when one of us was shocked by an unexpected death. And that's where I listened to Bert's great fear of not making medical school. And this must be ... I was feeling it all. But when Steven took my arm to move me on across the street I was back instantly. And I realized I did not wish the time back, though. I like my here and now life. Yet, it felt and feels ever so strange that none of us Munich crew stayed in our city. From all of us, actually I am the closest to it now – as far as I know. One is living at the Danube close to the Austrian border, one is a doctor in Northern Bavaria, one is probably in Latin America. Nothing lasts forever, is the slogan that would fit here. But it sure can be miserable as well when everything dissolves and you come back to a feeling of emptiness. And feel left behind. But not for long. I regained another part of this city. It does not make me feel any clearer about myself, though. Home must really be where the heart is, where else could it be?

Notes from the 48th North

Sent: Tuesday, 1 April 2014 ~ 1.44am

Yes, thank you, I am gladly coming with you. Getting out of here and strolling through Paris will do me good. I am longing to be an expat again. We are leaving on Tuesday evening? That is great because in that city one should arrive at night. I am going, packing now. Tuesday morning I am announcing that I am ready. I am enjoying my breakfast differently today. It is the anticipation. My head is already working out my first tour Wednesday morning. But for right now we have a peculiar problem and quite unexpectedly. Look at it, he calls out. I am watching the TV screen. It's the channel with the snow and weather reports for the Austrian and German Alps. You are kidding! One metre of fresh supply of powder? Blue skies? Should we go skiing instead? I want to go skiing, we both state. Yes, want but can't Steven says. Can't you ask to postpone that meeting? I mean Paris vs skiing is a very tough choice. But skiing has to win. Snow will melt but Paris will be there later. We contemplate, big-eyed, mischievously, fresh bun in hand mid air. Paris won out over the snow supply.

I am strolling through the back streets toward the Seine. I descend down to the cobble stone path right by the water. A cold wind blows and I pull up my hood. I walk under the bridges and on towards I don't know where. Just enjoy the foreign sounds around me. I used to live here once. I feel expat foreign, feel familiar and somewhat home. Weird. The line of people waiting for entrance to the d'Orsay museum are too long for me. I meander on. Somehow I come back to the hotel. And again it is night and it lures us out into the city for a night stroll. On one of the bridges we stand and look into the water of the river churned up by the boats speeding by. A little woolly dog, gray, black, and white excitedly sniffs around. He is just three months old the owner tells me. He is a Husky, also a foreigner here in Paris. He has to like cobble stone ways and forget putting his paws into snow.

The next day is a free day for Steven. We decided to be at the Louvre half an hour before they open the gates. We stand in a long line. I am patient out of an urge to see the master paintings again. And I have never been real close to Mona Lisa before. This time I am determined.

And I succeed. There she is, 500 years old, secured by double glass encasing. People take pictures, flashes are no longer forbidden. Tourists, I think. How come I don't feel like one? I feel like I belong here. Weird.

We visit a friend of Steven's in her office. Have a nice reunion.

Lebanese, married to a Swiss, living in Paris. That is just down my alley. An expat like me. Have a good trip back to Munich, she says. See you in Beirut, Isolde. Well, unlikely, but not entirely unlikely for an expat.

That felt good to me. Just like in olden days when I was still a true expat.

Notes from the 48th North

Sent: Saturday, 26 April 2014 ~ 11.06am

A few beautiful spring days ago I walked back into the village coming from the eastern forest. The second house to the right is usually empty and closed. But that day a man stood on a ladder sandpapering the wall. This is Hannes, I said to myself. How nice. Isolde, hello! he shouted at me from up there. We had a nice lengthy talk about being back home. We understood each other. It felt good to recall our common history and experiences in Egypt and Cairo in addition to thrashing out our home coming once again. For me it always means some continuity with people that once shared a stretch of my life. And being understood at eye level is healing to myself image. But as of lately that was not all of it.

One afternoon, three days after the above encounter with Hannes, I answered my phone. Isolde! a voice unknown to me almost whispered my name. No recognition, no recall, not even a hint. It's me, Anna, she helped me out. Anna, I repeated in surprise. Where are you? – a common and necessary question being asked amongst modern nomads. Here, in Nuernberg. I am finished in China, she explained. For good? This being another question reflecting frequent international moves. She is a friend I separated from in the hot desert summer of 2009 in Dubai. Now, after four years in Peking, she is back and looking for a job in the vicinity of northern Bavaria. I don't like it here, it is so boring, she tells me. And the people are so strange and unkind. In China I had a good ... Oh, good grief, Anna, she is in the rejection stage tilting towards a depression hole of home coming after so many years abroad. She is asking me to visit her in Nuernberg. Of course, I will. Having been apart many thousands of kilometres three hundred of them seem like a piece of cake. Neighborly!

At least some are back to touch base. Of course, we are aware that it will be a new or at least an adjusted base. Experience and years are interfering with connecting to the original base. But who would want to?

Being abroad for many years, expats evolve on. May I cite the author again that titled his book *You Can't Go Home Again*? Well, yes and no. You can, if you are willing to adjust your expectation of a revised and reshaped environment and friendships of once upon a time. I'll be off to Nuernberg soon.

Notes from the 48th North

Sent: Thursday, 1 May 2014 ~ 7.38pm

Bavaria celebrated itself today. And we were even blessed by the colors of our flag in the sky: white and blue.

On this day of the 1st of May it is tradition to set up a tree, a May tree, ein Maibaum. It has got at least two wreaths with a lot of colorful ribbons flapping in the wind. In the past we also hung sausages and chocolate hearts on it for the guys to climb up there and get them for their ladies. That practice we have dropped a long time ago though.

Nowadays Maibaeume (Baeume – plural for Baum) are smoothly painted, you guessed it, white and blue, and twenty-metres high. We are not sure what the reason for this exercise is. Some say it stems from heathen customs whereas science disputes this. But we agree amongst ourselves that we do it just for the heck of it, to have fun and get together.

One tradition we have kept though, lest the fun would be out the window. That "tree", being stored at some farmer's barn and in waiting for the 1st of May, has to be stolen from somebody. On 1st May the "thieves" bring it back with a lot of tamtam. They also have to put it up which is a case of hard physical labor. And in order to recover from that ordeal it is followed by beer, schnapps, and food, paid by the lucky village folks.

I was out there today from 11.00am on. Nothing was there yet. But I saw the fire engine-trucks blinking blue at the southern edge of the forest. The "tree" was stretched out horizontally and endlessly over two two-wheel vehicles. All the youth of the neighboring village was riding on the "tree", shouting, laughing, and yelling, and drinking guess what. Somebody played music which the tractor, pulling the whole vehicle, helped to spoil. Then they stopped shortly before the village sports field (where the tree will be located upright for the next two years). What's keeping you? I asked them. We ran out of Diesel, they said. Okay, I walked back to the destination meanwhile. On my way there I met the lady who was delivering the Diesel in small glasses, some with content as clear as water, others were golden colored. After that refreshment the tractor ran again.

Meanwhile the sports field had filled up with benches and tables and people. So many to talk to. So often I was questioned: Isolde, are you here alone, where is your husband? Beirut. Oh, my God, Richard exclaimed. Isn't it dangerous there? Then they started to push up the tree with so called swallows, meaning two long poles crossed close to the top and tied together there.

There they were, the combined youthful manpower of our neighbor village. First the tree needed to be put just right into the grass so that it will slip into a steel casing when it is finally up-right. Everybody wearing traditional leather pants, some hand embroidered, each one to the tune of 400 to 800 Euros. Employing the well tested method of "hau ruck (say how roock)" they started to lift the top end of the Maibaum off the ground, inching it upward more and more with more and more swallows put underneath. Richard had his huge tractor running from which a steel cable extended to the tree where it was hooked up to it. He stood there like the trust worthy forester he is with his remote control around his waist. It was his job to tighten the steel cable as they pushed the tree higher and higher. They had rests in between for drinking beer and smoking a cigarette. I mean a guy has to have nourishment to work so hard. And, yes, I must not forget, one of them had to talk to somebody on his mobile during the five minute break. I took a seat on a ladder leaning against the fire station house. After two hours our Maibaum stood there up-right, reaching into the white and blue Bavarian sky. The ribbons and the small flag on top waved gently in the wind. I went home with a camera full of pictures. Have not witnessed the raising of a Maibaum in decades – not with swallows anyway.

The event had gotten under my skin. Maybe that was a result from talking about our childhood there off and on practically for hours. In the evening I went back to look at it one more time. Don't know why. Of course, the Maibaum will be there for the next two years as testimony to old customs being alive and bringing people together to celebrate.

Notes from the 48th North

Sent: Wednesday, 21 May 2014 ~ 6.47am

Why does another one of my best friends have to leave? So her question appeared on Facebook anyway. Oh I understand where this is coming from, my dear friend. I have left you once behind, too. Was five years ago. I answered her extensively to help her out. That was yesterday. Last night I had one of those miserable nights that sometimes visit me. So at 4.00am I gave up and went to my computer. It always helps. At 4.30am his mobile alarm went off. Time to get up, pack the rest, drink a glass of water, and leave. It was as lovely and soothing a morning as can be. The air was warm enough to suggest a warm day, a warm summer. It felt mild in my face. A pale, pink streaked sky presented itself in romantic, mild, peaceful mood. Everything appeared mildly romantic. Only the many birds around our house were making a lot of noise. I mean the *tweet-tweet* noise. Excitedly they flew from one tree, from one bush to another. In the midst of that I stood in the morning breeze watching the tail lights of the taxi disappear. It was heading for the airport thereby making me ask that question polemic style, I have to admit. What was on the agenda today? Hopefully a lot for I feel left behind. I feel down, actually I feel like going somewhere myself like to a lake to swim. Or I could go back to bed and hibernate until he comes back. Stop that! It is not a first and it will happen again. Those who prevail shall inherit the earth.

Notes from the 48th North

Sent: Monday, 9 June 2014 ~ 10.53am

No matter how nice it tries to ring, it is still an ugly alarm clock with the purpose of waking up the sleeping. This morning though, I was already awake. Still, throw that thing out the window. But my determined husband had to be in London later in the morning. It was 4.45am and time to head for the airport. No coffee, no breakfast, just get out and drive off. By that time I had already sniffed the beautiful, early morning summer air of a promising day. It was daylight but with barely a sun ray over the eastern horizon. I am going to do my Nordic walk now. Yes, now! By a quarter to six I headed out the door. It was beautifully cool, silent, and light feeling after the hoopla of the historic tractors' day and the tremendous noise all day yesterday. I had thought about calling my walking partner. But then, one doesn't do that so early, right?

The dew drops sparkled in the sun which had cleared the horizon by now. An ever so light mist hung very low over the fields and meadows. The slugs were on their way to breakfast. One lone rabbit took off when I was still a distance away. It was so very still though. Only the birds negate my words completely. One big bird, one of the predators, scared me when I went through the forest with its wush-wush, wings. The sky was undisturbed blue, not one cloud anywhere. Not a frequent occurrence at this latitude. A song jumped into my mind: Oh what a beautiful morning, Oh what a beautiful day, I have this beautiful feeling, everything is going my way (from the musical *Oklahoma*).

But then I saw a plane coming from south-easterly direction, still without a sound audible. As I regretted the white condense water line it drew over the pristine sky I saw another one coming from due east, disturbing in the same way the flawless blue. And, yes, there appeared another one coming from the south east part of the world. They started somewhere at 2.00 or 3.00am to come in for one of the first landings in Munich (MUC airport has night flight prohibition). I was in one of those planes often times. So I wished them a happy landing and held my horses still. But today, these planes messed up my sky. Something else brought me back to inner peace, though, when I saw it also coming out of the south east. A hot air balloon – where did he take off so early in the am? Chiemsee, south of the Alps, Austria, Greece? It was soundless and did not draw lines into the pristine blue heavens. Well, the three planes I never heard either. They just crossed Munich airspace and raced on. What I did hear though was, besides the exited chirping of a multitude of bird species, the church bells of at least three churches from more or less neighboring villages. Their sounds came across crystal clear. It was different for each church. I can't think when I have heard that last. I still must have been a little girl. In those days, however, I did not consciously appreciate such early morning summer days. I didn't know then what I know now: They are precious happenings even if not everything goes my way. The sounds of their bells says home and stability to me!

Notes from the 48th North

Sent: Monday, 30 June 2014 ~ 6.18am

Every year I am looking forward to this concert. It is a highlight of a music summer between the Inn and Salzach rivers. This church as a venue is a treat in itself located on top of a hill and thus overlooking a valley of two rivers. It has no electricity in it and thus the second half of the concert is bathed in candle light. Consequently I did not look carefully through the program. And I paid for it. Otherwise I would have known that this was something for the music experts and theorists. Not the plain listeners like me.

I have never been a friend of Baroque music or a violin solo. It is okay occasionally. But spare me from two hours. Already the opener was a treat for some. Have you ever heard of a composer named Georg Muffat (lived somewhere between 1645–1704)? Well, I am glad I know about him now. I'll watch out for this guy in the future and avoid him when I can. It was a violin thing accompanied by an ancient cembalo. Clunc, clunc, clunc. The second sonata was from Carl Philipp Emanuel Bach, second son of Johann Sebastian, a cembalo solo. I don't know how the pianist could get a Moll out of that cembalo as I did not hear it. It must be my ears for sure. This was followed by Georg Friedrich Haendel's (1685–1759) Sonata for violin and cembalo. Okay, if it had to be.

Then came the intermission. Out into the grass we all went. Oh the sunset was marvelous with a reviving, regenerating, glorious view into the Alpine horizon. That is, I enjoyed it because I knew that this is where the Alps normally are visible if the evening haze allows them to come out.

What would you like, Isolde, some OJ or rather a glass of champagne? I need some alcohol please! For there will be more Baroque. And a violin solo on top! That one will hurt my ears and brain. A single violin is just screeching too much for me. Yes, I know, the virtuoso is a renowned from the Munich Philharmonic and he plays like an angel. But he cannot help for his instrument either. He normally plays the flute so wonderfully that I feel elated and satisfied in my music needs. How come today he plays the screecher? If he just had brought all the violinists of the Munich Phils! Now for that I would not need alcohol, rather I would be in the seventh musical heaven.

For the second half of this music event there were two Sonatas from Johann Sebastian Bach (1685–1750). No. 1 was that violin solo which was something for my listening skills. But – bravo, bravissimo virtuoso, its just that I did not study music and don't get the beauty of this into my right lobe of my neo-cortex. Yep, that's how theoretical I experience such a sonata. The Sonata No. 3 was for cembalo and violin and gave me a bit of peace at the end. The solo violin will go back to Munich and the cembalo will be packed carefully and driven back to the place Altenmarkt, a little city with a big old cathedral, also used for concerts. It is located exactly where the 48th parallel runs through.

And that is a good place, isn't it? Let's hope for that cembalo again next music summer and I do hope even more for that flute. Thanks, it was good education! So, how about you and Baroque music?

Notes from the 48th North

Sent: Saturday, 19 July 2014 ~ 7.40pm

It was one of those beautiful summer mornings featuring blue sky, a lovely ever so slight breeze, and a temperature that does not call for long sleeves. One layer of skimpy summer clothing is enough. In a light mood I walked to our neighborhood store for fresh bread. It was to come even nicer. A car stopped by my side. Both doors opened and out came our friends who lived in Cairo while we were there as well. Hi there, what a surprise! Yes it is, Brenda said. Yep, you are rarely visiting and spending time here long enough to share an evening. Well, we are at least four months out of the year in our house in Portugal. Then there is so much going on in Munich, and next week, Brenda explained, I am going home to Denmark to visit my folks. Yeah, that leaves hardly time for us here in Bavaria, Brenda. Shakers and movers you are still, aren't you? Well, what about you, you are just as rarely here, Isolde.

What, why would I? I live here. What do you mean you live here? I thought you are living in Dubai. Or did you not say Lebanon? Let's straighten this out, Brenda. I used to live in the Emirates, and Steven is mostly in Beirut. I have moved back here in 2009! I have been here for five years now! And you think I am still living elsewhere? Can't imagine you being stationary for good, Isolde. Try it for the future, Brenda.

It clearly was an issue between us: Where were we, where are we now? We both, or rather the four of us, have not ceased to think of each other as expats living somewhere abroad. Anywhere but at home.

So can we get together next week when Steven is back? Unfortunately no, they both said. They are going to Denmark. But, so they suggested, at the end of summer we could get together? Brenda looked at me intensely.

Unfortunately no, not yet. We are going to be overseas for a few weeks. Did somebody say we are finished with being elsewhere?

Notes from the 48th North

Sent: Wednesday, 22 October 2014 ~ 1.36am

Some noise woke me up. It was almost midnight. Thus it took me a while to recognize the racket for what it was. Something I have always liked. A fierce storm, actually the first fall storm this season, is blowing around the house. The shutters of four windows are rattling and whistling strongly and without a rest. But I hear another sound beneath and more in the background. It is a rumbling sound. An earthquake approaching? A tornado? The latter thought jolts me out of bed! Suddenly I hear sirens howling their ugly, anxiety-arousing warning. I am waiting for the fire engines to come blasting through our village. But zip, nothing! I settle down.

And on and on the storm blows relentlessly around the house. I am alone and therefore quite vigilant. After a while I begin to enjoy the symphony of the wind without anxiety. My mind wanders back to the time when I was at Scottsdale College in Arizona. I was also alone. My love had been in Iowa for weeks already. While there he composed a poem for me titled *The Cold Wind Rattles the Windows*. Very beautiful! Now it is my turn to compose. Fall Storm Rattling the Shutters? Storm North of the Alps? The Romantic Bavarian Nights? They all would be good subjects and titles. But I opt for the immediate stimulation: Storm Symphony Poem from the 48th North.

He (masculine in German) is a fierce beauty of sound, He rattles the shutters with fury,

He will dump snow down to 700 metres.

He will make me change my summer tires on my car, Sepp. Can you change my tires this week?

The cold wind rattles the windows gently by now. The Symphony of Storm in the fall.

Notes from the 48th North

Date: Sunday, 4 January 2015 ~ 6.12am

It is 4.45am when the gentle sound of the iPhone alarm sounds. In fifteen minutes the taxi will be turning around in our driveway heading towards the airport route. I get up to have a look out the window to check the weather and road conditions this winter morning. The barn has a beautiful ring of light around the roof. That's where the sun is peeking over the horizon in January. It also illuminates long stretched storm clouds making them look beautifully threatening. Yep, "beautiful" and "threatening" can go together! There comes the interfering but welcome blinking orange light of the huge winter service vehicle of the Municipality spraying salt onto the frozen waters on the roads. I hug my traveler goodbye. Let me know when you have reached the airport safely. And then when you arrive in Beirut and the +25C warmth there. Say hello to my friend. Happy and safe journey to you! I shall hold down the fort.

It occurs to me that I have just done the same two days ago. Only then he and I took our son to the same airport. The salt truck also just went in front of us to prevent the rain from freezing a sheet of sparkling black ice over the road. The winter had remembered us just the day after Christmas. There was no skiing time anymore, the avalanche warnings and the bad colds that we just had gone through (and still counting) notwithstanding.

So now I am challenged once again to fill the void of an empty looking all too quiet house. I know I am not the only one in this by any means. Just look at my Facebook page! I'll apply my strategy of fitness training, weather permitting as outdoors is much more soul liberating to me than indoors. And often I meet like-minded people. Yesterday Chris, the fitness trainer, was standing on the sheet of ice over the lake by the north side of the forest. Will it hold twenty people for the Bavarian version of curling? And then he jogged on in front of me, uphill, without slowing a lick showing me how it is done. See, I am feeling better already.

Thank you for listening once again. Don't give the post-holiday blues a chance. It will pass. In this sense I wish you a very good start into 2015. We shall be talking. Please!

Notes from the 48th North

Date: Thursday, 5 March 2015 ~ 4.44pm

You remember that I have often agonized here about the many wonderful people I have lost or at least had to leave behind as I moved on to other cities and countries. With some it was so painful a loss that I am still feeling it after all this time. Some I have had the luck to be able to visit. But to my great pleasure and healing some have resurfaced! Also: After all this time! Those are the jewels that can stay close over distance and time. Like this one ...

Last September he (and his partner) drove for hours in a car to meet us in Oregon. It was like we had never been apart. The decades of not meeting seemed to have vanished. But we separated again putting continent and ocean between us. But lo and behold this February, about five months after our reunion in Oregon, he sent an email. *Guess what! I'll be in Madrid in a week or so*, he said without pathos. Of course, why not, he is of the traveling kind? We're going to meet somewhere? You bet my dear friend out of Berkeley. I did not forget you are from the Berkeley crew as well, a kind of personality like no other. I am going to be in Erlangen in Germany in two days to see my play *The Wave*, he wrote. After that I told him to visit Nuernberg. He did (and his partner). But they went on to Munich the same day and then on to Salzburg and back to Munich. Europe in three days! Yep, then Steven picked him up at our little train station. And here he was on our farm in southern Bavaria. As I said, it was as if we had just left each other yesterday and now will pick up our conversation from Oregon and keep going. A shaker and a mover he is, always has been, this delightfully mobile person. Well, don't rest just yet. He (and his partner) we put on a train, the same day, to go to Innsbruck, Austria. But it was the wrong train. The conductor told them to go back to our train station and take the right train for this special ticket to go to Innsbruck. Eventually he (and his partner) arrived there. But the next day the weather was too ghastly and winterish. What to do? Yep, move on the same morning to go to Zurich, Switzerland. That's were I lost track of him. Somehow he (and his partner) took a train to Munich. Next day on to Madrid to catch the plane that would take him (and his partner) back over said ocean and continent to the far away Pacific Northwest. Yep, we have an email each confirming that they arrived back home safely. You figure they are spinning on their own axis by now? Not them, I guess!

Is that a whirlwind or what? Perhaps these are the friends that resurface, the travelers, like me. Yes, we intend to visit again, either here or there. Thank you for brushing by Mark and Lisa. These *Notes from the 48th North* are dedicated to you.

Notes from the 48th North

Date: Friday, 29 May 2015 ~ 1.33am

Try as I might I cannot fall asleep tonight. An event that happened today is going around in my head like a windmill. I have to write it out of my mind – and send it to you. Thank you.

An 88-year-old man had passed away. His funeral was yesterday, Thursday.

He was the last of two men of this community, this village, who had been soldiers in the dying days of the Second World War. That means he was eighteen years old when the war ended. He made it back home in one piece. From two of my long-gone uncles I learned that the highlight of those veterans is to die at home in their own bed as opposed to, say, in the steppes of Russia. Well, that wish was granted to this man. Now we have one more, the last one, of a soldier who was in the hellish days of WWII. He is 90-years old. Also was a teenager in war. I spoke to him about war issues a few times when I needed help with the story I was working on. He was at the funeral to see his comrade put to rest.

Reserve hat Ruh – reserves can rest. I wonder what he might have felt watching the funeral and particularly when the three shots salute were fired. It always seemed to me a questionable thing to do to honor somebody with three canon shots over the grave when they had heard them for years as a the threat to their lives. Wouldn't silence be more desirable a thing for them?

And on it goes. Just a few days ago they found a five-kilogram bomb when digging down for some repair work in northern Germany. It was laying under a school!

I'll try to sleep now. Thanks for listening. Hope I did not spoil your day. Tomorrow there will be another more amusing (hopefully) event: Munich's second soccer team, 1860 Muenchen, will battle for staying in the second league. You see, the previous generation players, some of them at least, went to English classes with me. They were nice guys. Yep, you guessed it, it was a matter of falling in and out of love. It was a nice time. May their successors fair well. Good night!

Notes from the 48th North

Date: Saturday, 6 June 2015 ~ 11.48am

The weatherman was threatening thunderstorms, rain showers without thunder and dropping temperatures already yesterday. Still I had a most pleasant, solo, morning Nordic walking time. The walking was unusually easy uphill. Had to be repeated today. At 6.30am I was out with my poles. But it was not as easy today, not like floating. Like yesterday the sky was what the Italians call "azzuro". Only the planes disturbed the pristine blue. I could see five planes with one glance yesterday, each making a line across. But today (of course I was earlier) there was not even that. Not one of them, not even a small Cessna, not even a model airplane with remote control. Ha, the G7 conference in the Alps is good for something!

A gentle, cool air blew around me. It felt so good. So did the silence. Silence, that means the birds were so loud as if they had a breakfast meeting. But not one person was crossing my path, not even the usual dog walkers were out. The various grasses waving in the wind were pretty high already to the benefit of those breeding on the ground. They, though, let me know that I am not exactly welcome in their territory.

When I crossed my favorite, lovely creek a pheasant angrily took off right next to me. Almost scared me to death. A few metres further down the path two deer jumped out of the grass and fled in big leaps. Scared me to death, too. But the overgrown, fat cat sitting in my path watching me approach was not a scare at all. A strange cat though. Well, as I came a few steps closer she stood up, walked on in a dignified way and sat down again staring at me. Then she stood up, turned to leave, turned back again to take another look at me and started to run in small steps. She had a huge bushy tail, reddish color, black ears, beautiful. She was a baby fox! I have seen foxes before, but not babies. Then one jump and she (perhaps he) was in the long grass and gone. Should have been a bit more weary of that one.

I came home in good spirits. A song came to my mind from "Porgy and Bess": "Summertime and the livin' is easy". That opera has always had a place in my heart for more than one reason. One of them is certainly Porgy's declaration of love to Bess. It reminds me of a woman of my acquaintance who was asked (in the wild sixties) Shall we throw our stuff together? Meaning, do you want to marry me? And another one I know. Her man sent this in the time of cyberspace and internet and smart phones, an SMS saying, Sorry, can't marry you. Of course, there are these three words all over the world that could be used for a proposal: *I love you*. But Porgy was original and overly tender with Bess, you are my woman now.

I did change subject now, didn't I? Have a good day, my friends and use those three words. I love you, too.

Notes from the 48th North

Date: Monday, 22 July 2015 ~ 2.38pm

My laundry program I used ran for one hour and fifty-seven minutes at 75C. It contained at least two ounces of sud for heavy dirt. When I took the washed items outside to dry I shook out one of Papa's white T-shirts. Would you believe it, out fell a bumble bee! She was a bit drowsy I think. She crawled away slowly. She did not fly. After that she was seen no more.

The insects certainly will outlive the human race.

Any comments my dear National Geographics watchers?

Notes from the 48th North

Date: Friday, 24 July 2015 ~ 1.34am

The last two weeks or more at this latitude in central Europe we had what we think classifies as unusually hot summer temperatures. That is temps above and beyond 32, 33 degrees C. At +35C we consider it unbearable. It keeps us sleepless. But higher than that we quit functioning properly. In response to such weather challenges firefighters in Austria had an idea ...

It happened in upper Austria at a refugee camp. Those refugees had come from countries beyond the Near and Middle East. Living in tents is not nice at the best of times much less at very high temps. The firefighters took one of their huge trucks and drove it to that camp. Then they rolled out their hoses of considerable diametre and turned on the water. White water sprays were raining down to the burnt earth and the little kids living there. They ran fully clothed, boys and girls, into the fountains from the blue skies. They jumped, turned, danced, rolled in the puddles and generally screeched with delight. They did what kids do: play and be silly when it is called for. All pain and terror and angst forgotten for a while. All suspicions of differences left behind, hands and minds overcame fear of what is not understood and reached out from one people to another. Just a little thinking and understanding and a little lovin'. What wonderful healing it did! Bless those firefighters!

Notes from the 48th North

Date: Sunday, 4 October 15 ~ 11.11am

It was a rational discussion conducted in a courteous manner about the pros and cons of teaching a foreign language to early childhood pupils. Quite a pleasant affair until one young educator suggested to do away with mandatory cursive writing classes. That caused some of the group members to raise their voices talking in a much more animated fashion as to the impossibly false idea presented. When the young teacher than dished out his reasoning of the computerization of the academic world or any world for that matter, and consequently the absence of any need to write by hand he brought down the group to a less dignified behavior of discussion.

As for me having watched or read not the first time such a subject matter being analyzed, I am in disbelief of such a futuristic thinking. Occasionally this issue has come up between my son and me. Sometimes when visiting he has seen me jotting down some notes on a piece of paper. His reaction came promptly, trying to convince me that I have to join the modern computerized world. You have a phone, don't you, Mama? As with the discussion above and my son's efforts to change me to taking my notes on my iPhone I have imagined a world without handwriting. Well, I fail to imagine it possible. This is to say: It makes me shudder. I find a piece of paper lighter in my pocket and easier to access than my mobile or my computer. The latter I find more cumbersome for the issues at hand.

To put more fire on the inflamed point of no cursive writing, let me repeat to you a short story. One of my acquaintances was getting ready to get married to her love of a few years. However, a few weeks or maybe months before, she received an SMS from said love informing her that the wedding is off as well as the whole relationship. Full stop! I never asked how many words or abbreviations he had used. How about that? Further proof that no cursive writing skills are needed anymore. That makes me look at the good old love letter, once upon a time, handwritten and with a drop of perfume in the paper. Or just a letter to a friend. It used to be understood as almost an insult, at least very impersonal though, to write such literature with a type writer. Should we write e-lovs? Well, yes, I admit it is better than none. But is it not nice to have something in your hands that your loved one has touched before, where his or her hand has been sliding across?

I don't know where you stand on this issue. But I do know the handwritten notes I have received from some. And yes, I have all my letters that my mother once wrote to me. And she has left me her love letters she had received from my father. Yes, I have also received love letters. Rarely do I pull them out to reread them on a rainy day. But if I wanted to I could. It still would be the paper that was in the hands of the author. And did you know that here you can hire somebody to have a love letter written in your name. It costs Euro 16,99. How did it come out to .99? BTW, I define love letter quite liberally and widely. If you are ever in need of one I will send you one at no cost, but lovingly. Take care, thanks for listening.

Also by Isolde Martin ...

This book is not fiction. This is the story of the author's life as an expatriate, and takes the reader on a journey through five continents and seven countries. In her frequent moves from country to country and from continent to continent, the author invites the reader to share the pleasures, the richness, the personal gains, and the high emotional costs of such a nomadic lifestyle for her and her family. The author details her struggles to adjust as she learns to live in each culture, experiencing both blunders and successes. She explores her journey towards integrity and inner balance, and shares her growth as a person. This is a story about the psychological, social and cultural effects of a modern nomadic life. The author's own story illustrates and clarifies the psychological processes at work. Those who have lived under such circumstances or those who are embarking in it now can learn to understand and perhaps even anticipate their own responses better and thus master the stress of international life more successfully.

www.ingramcontent.com/pod-product-compliance
Lightning Source LLC
Chambersburg PA
CBHW070559300426
44113CB00010B/1326